UP, UP AND AWAY

UP, UP AND AWAY

*How we found love, faith, and a lasting
marriage in the entertainment world*

**by Marilyn McCoo and Billy Davis, Jr.
with Mike Yorkey**

NORTHFIELD PUBLISHING
CHICAGO

All Scripture quotations, unless otherwise indicated, are taken from the Holy Bible, New International Version®. NIV®. Copyright © 1973, 1978, 1984 by International Bible Society. Used by permission of Zondervan Publishing House. All rights reserved.

Scripture quotations marked TLB are taken from The Living Bible. Copyright © 1971. Used by permission of Tyndale House Publishers, Inc., Wheaton, Illinois 60189. All rights reserved.

Scripture quotations marked NKJV are taken from the New King James Version. Copyright © 1982 by Thomas Nelson, Inc. Used by permission. All rights reserved.

Library of Congress Cataloging-in-Publication Data

McCoo, Marilyn.
  Up, up and away : How we found love, faith, and a lasting marriage in the entertainment world / by Marilyn McCoo and
Billy Davis, Jr. with Mike Yorkey.
      p. cm.
  Includes bibliographical references and index.
  ISBN 1-881273-17-2
  1. McCoo, Marilyn. 2. Davis, Billy, Jr. 3. Musicians—United States—Biography. I. Davis, Billy, Jr. II. Yorkey, Mike. III. Title.
  ML420.M1298A3 2004
  782.42164'092'2—dc22

                                                    2004014618

ISBN: 1-881273-17-2

1 3 5 7 9 10 8 6 4 2

Printed in the United States of America

CONTENTS

Introduction

So many people have approached us over the years asking us to write a book, especially about our marriage. As we celebrated our 25th and then 30th anniversaries, they marveled at how we were able to do it. How were two people in our chosen profession, with all of the temptations, the opportunities for indulging our wildest fantasies, able to stick to a commitment made to each other? The promise " 'til death do us part" seems to have lost its meaning a long time ago and is now treated as merely part of the nuptial routine, like the tossing of the bridal bouquet after the ceremony.

To tell you the truth, we too feel wonder at the number of years we've been together, well over half of both of our lives. No one really expected us to make it this far. The 5th Dimension group members, family, and many close friends—while wanting to share in our joy and the excitement of two people committing their lives to each other—silently wondering how long this would last and what disasters lay ahead.

We could not talk about our relationship without including the amazing experience of being part of a phenomenon, a singing group which hit suddenly and hit big, beginning in the late Sixties and continuing into the Seventies. So many things impacted our lives. Actually, without the 5th Dimension, there would probably be no "us". We know many of you will remember, if not the exact moments, the times and mood of those years— the styles, the mind-set. Florence, Lamonte, Ronald, and we were caught up in a whirlwind. It was one of the most incredible times of our lives, full of experiences too fantastic to have even dreamed about. We are eternally grateful for those wonderful years and adventures and are happy to share some of the highlights with you.

We have not written the definitive account of our years with the 5th Dimension. For one thing, that was not our intention. We are providing these stories as a backdrop of our relationship. Second, we can only tell them from our own perspective. We are sure the other group members have their versions to tell, along with the exciting new experiences from their ongoing successful careers.

We have no fool-proof formula to offer for a successful union. We can only share with you our joys and struggles, the challenges we've confronted that sometimes made it seem like we might not make it this far. Our hope is that those of you who may find yourselves faced with problems not too different from those we've encountered will be encouraged. We often think that our troubles are unlike anyone else's and no one would understand. When we learn that we are more alike than different, it relieves a burden. When we find that others have found solutions that we felt were unsolvable, it gives us new energy to try again.

That's what we hope to accomplish with our story, and we hope you'll enjoy the trip down memory lane in the process. It was so much fun reliving these experiences.

Marilyn McCoo & Billy Davis, Jr.

"My thoughts turned back to those exciting days in the mid-1960s, when I was introduced to this wild young singer from St. Louis . . ."

CHAPTER 1

(LAST NIGHT)
I DIDN'T GET TO SLEEP AT ALL

*I couldn't close my eyes 'cause
you were on my mind . . .*

August 27, 1999 ~ *Cedars-Sinai Medical Center in Los Angeles*

Marilyn McCoo: For the daughter of two doctors, it always surprised me that I never got used to the antiseptic smell of a hospital corridor—or the waiting around. Perhaps that's why the slow ticktock passage of time in the waiting room wore on my nerves. The uncertainty of what was happening in a Cedars-Sinai surgical bay caused my mind to contemplate thoughts that I had never entertained before.

The thought of losing my husband, Billy, who had just turned sixty-one, boggled my mind. People die in their seventies and eighties, not in their early sixties when they're strong as bulls and still in good health. When Billy received the news two months earlier that he had prostate cancer, my world reeled in disbelief. Cancer always happened to someone else, not *my* family. I was suddenly forced to confront the very real possibility that I might have to live without Billy unless modern medicine could defeat this deadly foe.

The plan today, according to his physician Dr. Stuart Holden, was to perform a prostatectomy—the removal of the prostate. We had been forewarned that the operation could render Billy impotent and/or incontinent, and my husband had signed reams of "informed consent" papers acknowledging those possibilities. Although surgical techniques that did not disturb the nerve bundles had vastly improved, Dr. Holden said he could not rule out the possibility that Billy might come out of the surgery an impotent man. I had never seen Billy look so nervous after he gulped down that bit of news.

We had sought out Dr. Holden after an annual physical revealed that Billy's PSA levels—or prostate-antigen test—had shot up to eighteen, a number nearly off the chart. The number we wanted was anything under five. Dr. Holden, who had a gold-plated reputation among urological surgeons in the Los Angeles area, was the medical director of the Louis Warschaw Prostate Cancer Center at the Cedars-Sinai Medical Center. He had operated on dozens of prostate cancer victims in the entertainment community.

Now our surgery date with Dr. Holden had arrived, and I found myself pacing up and down the hospital corridor, worried sick that the doctor would find his body ravaged by cancer. My hope was that my husband could expect a normal life span.

When time slows down, as it did that morning, you have time to think. Thirty years of marriage with Billy flashed by like freeway mile markers. My thoughts turned back to those exciting days in the mid-1960s, when I was introduced to this wild young singer from St. Louis . . .

"Putting on those

silky white robes

and standing in front of

the congregation just

singing my heart out—

I loved doing that."

CHAPTER 2

POOR SIDE OF TOWN

*I can't blame you for tryin', I'm
tryin' to make it too . . .*

Billy Davis, Jr.: They say every good story starts at the beginning, and my story begins on June 26, 1938, when I was born in St. Louis, Missouri, where piano player Scott Joplin composed his ragtime classics at the turn of the century.

Work was hard to find in those post-Depression years, and many black families barely scraped by. My parents, Bill and Norris Davis, managed under such trying circumstances. I was born the sixth of seven children; I had three brothers (Arthur and Wilbert were older and Ronald was younger) and three sisters (Norzora, Velura, and Fedora were all older). We lived in a four-family flat: two families upstairs, two families downstairs.

My parents certainly had a handful to raise, and Daddy was an entrepreneur type who had gone into the lumber business with his brother, Ed. They opened the Davis Brothers Coal and Lumber Yard in South St. Louis and would go out into the woods near St. Charles to cut down trees and truck them to a mill in East St. Louis. They also hand-chopped wood, which they would stack into a huge pile at their lumber yard and sell to families heating their homes with wood stoves. My brothers and I were expected to help out, so we worked in the woods clearing away slash or throwing cordwood into the back of the truck for delivery.

I enjoyed working at a young age. I loved going out into the woods with Daddy and Uncle Ed and watching them cut down big trees. I was too young to swing a heavy axe, but they usually found something useful for me to do. One time when I was nine or ten years old, I was just itching to drive the delivery truck.

"When do I get to drive?" I pestered my brother.

"What makes you think you can drive this here truck?" Arthur said. "You have to be able to shift gears, you know." Arthur then shifted the large gearshift to impress me.

"Hey, I can do that!" I said. "You lemme drive."

"Okay, but don't say I didn't warn you," Arthur said. "This should be fun to watch."

I don't know how my feet reached the pedals, and I'm sure I could barely see over the dashboard, but I wanted to drive that truck in the worst way. Arthur explained how I had to ease off the clutch as I applied gas to the engine. I popped the clutch out, the truck lurched forward, and we were on our way. My excitement turned to panic, however, as I realized I didn't know how to stop this one-ton beast.

"Slow down!" my brother screamed, as we shot through the woods at a good clip.

Suddenly, a tree appeared out of nowhere. "How do you—" I jerked the steering wheel to the right and drove us off the road and into a ditch.

Daddy chewed out Arthur and me that night, leaving us with a strong reminder never to do that again. I've always remained close to Arthur following that incident, and we still tease each other about it to this day. I maintain he was a lousy driving instructor.

Daddy and Mother, when they weren't keeping up with our antics, made sure we went to church every Sunday. We attended a church a few doors down called the True Vine Spiritual Church. From as young as I can remember, I sang in the choir. Putting on those silky white robes and standing in front of the congregation just singing my heart out—I loved doing that.

But I was puzzled when one day—I must have been ten or eleven years old—my parents told us kids, "We're sick and tired about you all complaining about going to church every Sunday. So we think it's time we stop making you go to church because we don't want to put our religion on you. You can go out and find your own religion and follow what you think makes sense."

My three older sisters took my parents up on that, and they began attending a Roman Catholic church. Naturally, my younger brother and I followed them, and eventually we all got baptized and later confirmed as Catholics. Our congregation was racially mixed—black and white, which was unusual for the late 1940s and early 1950s, but being kids, we didn't make anything of it. I didn't like going to confession and telling the priest my sins, though, because I was a troublemaker. I can still remember how each confession started: "Bless me, Father, for I have sinned . . ."

As I got older, this confession thing wasn't making sense to me. What if I confessed my sins and the priest dropped dead before he got my sins up to the Father in heaven? Then I would be in a heap of trouble. Another thing I didn't like about the Catholic church was that they didn't have a choir, and I loved to sing. So when I started high school, I stopped going to the Catholic church and started attending a Baptist church because they had a great choir. I loved singing those old-time gospel songs, and I didn't mind singing those old standards for *hours* during the Sunday morning praise and worship time.

I had attended an all-black grammar school as a youngster, and when I reached the high school years, I moved on to Washington Technical High School, another all-black school. Integration was still a few years off. Washington Technical was a trade school, which is a fancy way of saying that they offered a lot of classes in auto shop, sheet metal shop, wood shop, or auto mechanic shop. Sure, I had my history, science, and biology classes, but my focus was on learning a trade, so I took sheet metal shop. What I really lived for at Washington Technical, however, was singing in the school choir.

I had loved singing ever since I was six years old. When I graduated from the first grade, my teacher organized a big performance for all the parents. I remember my teacher asking if anyone could sing, and I shot my hand into the air. I sang in church, and I could hold a tune very well for someone my age. So I sang "Oh, Bury Me Not on the Lone Prairie" at my first-grade graduation, and I will never forget it. My high-pitched voice was so pure, and I believed I could sing that song better than anyone who had before.

The teachers loved my performance, and my parents beamed with pride. Afterward, I overheard other adults telling my parents, "Billy can sing—he's good!" That's what I wanted to hear—praise.

When I reached high school, I wanted to do more than just sing in church on Sundays. I wanted to *entertain* people. I started singing in these little groups, but half the time my singing buddies didn't show up at my house to practice. I did a lot of waiting around. I wanted them to be as dedicated as I was, but they weren't.

To help pass the time, I started teaching myself to play the guitar. *Maybe this will take the place of my group,* I thought. I learned certain chords to play and sang to myself while I strummed my guitar. At least that was one way I could sing when no one showed up for practice.

I won a talent show my freshman year of high school, and boy, my head swelled. I knew I was cool. I remember all the girls pointing me out as I walked through the halls as though I was some big man on campus. One of those girls was a senior, and when she blinked her pretty eyes at me, we started going together. The senior guys didn't like a scrub freshman taking out a senior one bit, so I had an interesting time dealing with that.

I also had to deal with another incident my freshman year. On the last day of school, I wore nice pants, nice shoes, a nice sweater over my dress shirt—and a new straw hat. After the last school bell rang, I walked up Franklin Avenue to catch a streetcar when suddenly I was surrounded by a bunch of guys from that neighborhood. Today, we would call them gangbangers; but back then, they were just a regular gang called the Downtown Turks. I was fresh blood to them, so they jumped me because I was from another area of town.

They taunted me for the way I dressed, and one of them took my new hat and stepped all over it. Then they grabbed me and dragged me to a walkway between two buildings. I figured they were fixin' to give me a good beating. They threw me to the ground and started kicking me, but I bunched myself into a ball to protect myself while they pummeled me for all I was worth. They busted my lip, but that was about the extent of my injuries. Suddenly, they dispersed, and I don't know why. I escaped unharmed.

I was growing up fast—and about to grow up a lot faster. One afternoon, Daddy was working in the woods with a crew. They didn't have chainsaws in those days, which meant they had to chop down trees with double-bladed axes. One lumberjack swung his axe to take a big whack at a tree trunk, but suddenly the steel blade flew off the top of the axe handle. The double-edged blade sliced through the air like a saucer and struck my dad in the head. It's a wonder he wasn't killed right there, but his head gushed blood like the Mississippi River in springtime. The work crew rushed him to the hospital, where a doctor sewed him up—thirty or forty stitches in all.

That accident put Daddy out of commission for a while, but arthritis had been slowing him down anyway. I had an older sister, Velura, going to college, and another sister, Fedora, graduating from high school who *wanted* to go to college. It was then that I realized I would have to stop going to school and help the family, but that didn't bother me much because I wasn't looking to go to college.

I was seventeen years old at the time, and I already knew what I wanted to do with my life. I was going to be a singer, and I knew what I had to do to get there.

But those dreams would have to wait because the family expected me to work and contribute to keeping food on the table. So I quit school after my junior year and got a job working for a landscaping company. I made pretty good money laying down sod and putting in gardens in the white people's homes.

By now, I was feeling grown-up because I was out of school and working full-time. I had a girlfriend at the time—her name was Edna, and we had been going steady for a year or so. We met at a party through some friends, and she was only a month older than I was. I liked her because she was fun to be around. I was always looking for a good time, which was easy to find because I had started drinking by then.

I must confess that Edna had a cute figure as well, and she was built up real nice. All the guys liked her; she was a prize catch. We were a pair of teenagers who thought we loved each other, although at age seventeen, we had no idea what that meant. Nor did I have an idea about all these hormones swirling around inside me, but I *did* know that I wanted to mess around with her, if you catch my drift. To do that, I figured we should be married.

We got married at the end of the summer, two seventeen-year-olds setting up house in a little apartment a few miles west of my folks' home. I worked my landscaping jobs by day and played in a little band at night. Don't forget, I had taught myself to play the guitar, and as we moved into 1956, this cat named Elvis Presley was starting to make some noise with the release of his single "Heartbreak Hotel." I liked this new thing they were calling "rock 'n' roll," but young black guys like myself were drawn more to R&B, or rhythm 'n' blues.

My friends and I—we called ourselves the Emeralds—got booked into small nightclubs, playing the popular songs of the time: "Get a Job" by the Silhouettes, "Let's Dance" by Chris Montez, "Moonlight Bay" by the Drifters, and "All Shook Up" by Elvis Presley, among others. We later changed our musical direction and our name to the Saint Gospel Singers. In those days, if you sang to the accompaniment of piano and organs, you were "gospel," while "jubilee" singers sang with guitars or created their own harmonies and rhythms.

This was a great training ground, learning how to perform and sing in front of an audience. Then my father and I went into business together and purchased the Havana Club on Kings Highway. I worked there six nights a week and performed at least two or three of those nights each week.

Then in 1961, the "Berlin Crisis" hit the front pages of the *St. Louis Post-Dispatch*. The Russians were building a wall around West Berlin to keep those living in East Berlin from escaping to the West. This was the height of the Cold War, and tensions ran high between the Soviet Union and the United States.

Uncle Sam was drafting men into the army, and they were grabbing everybody they could—including married guys like me. Even Elvis Presley had to serve a two-year hitch from 1958 to 1960. After I finished basic training at Fort Chaffee, Arkansas, I was transferred to Fort Knox in Kentucky, where I went to school to become a turret mechanic— working inside tanks on the turret mechanism.

After six months, I was shipped out to West Germany—just like Elvis. I wanted to keep my music going, but I didn't know how that was going to happen in Europe. When I arrived at our base outside Nuremberg, I hooked up with four other black guys—the only other black guys in our company. We were naturally drawn to each other, and we enjoyed hanging around the barracks and griping about army life. One time, we hadn't gotten paid for weeks because of some typical army snafu, so we didn't have any money.

"Did you hear about the talent show they're having on base?" asked one of my buddies, a guy named Clayton.

"No, I haven't," I replied.

"I hear they're paying twenty bucks to the winner."

"Twenty bucks? I'm going to win this talent show so we can have some money," I declared.

I borrowed a guitar and sang "Save the Last Dance for Me," which the Drifters had just released. I brought the house down and won $20, which doesn't sound like much, but that would be like winning $200 today. I shared the money with my buddies. We used the winnings to purchase razor blades and toiletries, and whatever was left over, we spent on good German beer.

Whenever my buddies and I lifted a beer stein, they said I should form a music group to entertain the GIs. I put my feelers out, and since I won the talent show, it wasn't hard to find some guys to play with me. I became the front man for a little group we called "The Kingsmen." We began singing on weekends at the EM Club on base—the Enlisted Men's Club. We drew good crowds because there wasn't much for American GIs to do in West Germany. When word got out about our five-man combo, we were soon asked to play in the NCO Club (for noncommissioned officers) *and* the Officer's Club. We found ourselves singing several nights a week and doing matinee shows on the weekend. Overnight I was making more money *singing* in the army than *being* in the army.

I was the entrepreneur type, just like my father, and I saw an opportunity for us to expand our horizons. I found this second-rate club in Nuremberg—I think it was named the Rendezvous—with a stage and a big dance floor. The Rendezvous didn't have much going for it, so I approached the German owner and said I had an idea that could make us both some money. My German consisted of *bratwurst* and not much more, but through sign language and my limited vocabulary, I told him how we could pack the place with GIs and the local *frauleins* looking for something to do on a Sunday afternoon. German girls *loved* black music, I said, and I bragged that I was like a Pied Piper to them, hoping he'd understand the connection.

The German man just smiled at me, so I knew he wasn't understanding much of anything I was saying—except for the word "dollars." When I wrote some numbers on a piece of paper, he pointed at them and said, "Ja, ja," a lot. A handshake later, and we were in business together.

By this time, Edna had flown over to join me in Germany. She was working at the PX on base, and she made sure she got the word out that the Kingsmen would be playing at the Rendezvous because they were hot!

As I predicted to the German owner, we packed the house. I remember singing one time and looking out at the dance floor, where a whole lot of shakin' was going on. I looked over at the German owner and gave a little wave, and he smiled back to me. I'm sure he liked counting those receipts after each show. The Kingsmen became very popular with the GIs, and this was my first successful foray into show business. We had a great run, but when my hitch in Germany was over after eighteen months, I was ready to go home.

I returned on a troop ship with so many GIs on board that I thought the ship would sink. We were stacked in sleeping quarters like cordwood, and what I remember about the trip was all the guys getting seasick. They were hanging over the railing and retching, then lying down on the deck and moaning for hours. They didn't know it's best to keep your stomach full when you're out to sea.

One day, I must have skipped a meal because man, did I get seasick. It was one of the worst feelings—light-headed, dizzy . . . just awful. I stayed sick the rest of the trip, but seeing the Statue of Liberty as we arrived in New York harbor brightened my attitude. It felt great to be home.

I hung around New York for about a month. The Kingsmen had scattered after I left Germany, but I heard about some other guys from White Plains, New York, who were looking for a front man. I said I'd sing with them, and since we were in New York . . . why don't we see if the Apollo would book us? The Apollo, located on West 125th in Harlem, was known as the place "where stars are born and legends are made." The Apollo Theater introduced its world-famous "Amateur Night" back in 1934, and many stars, including Ella Fitzgerald, broke in at the Apollo.

I picked up a phone and said rather boldly, "This is Billy Davis, Jr., and I'm passing through New York with my group. We would like to see if we could do a performance."

"You're passing through New York?" said the friendly voice. "Why don't you come by and try out for our Amateur Night?"

That sounded fine with me. Remember, this was long before shows like *Star Search* or *American Idol*, so if you wanted to be "discovered" in the early 1960s, you had to play at the Apollo and keep winning the Amateur Night so you would be invited back the following week. That got your attention. Well, we won the night I sang at the Apollo. Afterward, I remember a one-armed man walking up to me and saying, "You win a few more weeks, and you could get a recording contract."

But I was out of money—and I had an anxious wife waiting for me back in St. Louis, so I couldn't stick around. I took a train home and got a job at the Scullins steel mill, which was hard work. I worked a day shift and played my guitar and sang in clubs at night, playing with different bands. One day, I had enough of blast furnaces, so I walked off the job. I believed I could support Edna and myself through my budding singing career, and I wanted to get back into the nightclub business.

My father and I purchased our second club together—called Club Oriole—and I got another band together. We didn't have a name, but my band played the latest dance music, covering such songs like "Under the Boardwalk" by the Drifters, "If You Need Me, Call Me" by Solomon Burke, and "The Twist" by Chubby Checker. We also traveled to different clubs in the St. Louis area and in neighboring Illinois, and sometimes we opened for great singers like Sam Cooke, Dinah Washington, and Louis Jordan. I was gone so much—and drinking with my band night after night. Edna and I began having marital problems. She wanted me to get a "regular job" with regular benefits. After six months of bitter arguing and fighting, we agreed to separate, although we had a young son named Steven, who was born in 1964.

Meanwhile, I pursued music. My grandfather, Phil Davis, was one of my biggest fans. He told me I was a good singer and that I should be "making records. "You can't do that living in St. Louis," he said. "St.

Louis has many things to offer, but we don't have record companies. You have to go to Detroit or Los Angeles."

Papa, my grandfather, got me thinking. I didn't know anyone in Detroit, but I knew someone in Los Angeles. An acquaintance, Lamonte McLemore (who dated my sister Fedora a few years earlier), had left St. Louis to check out the West Coast. Lamonte loved photography and took his Hasselblad camera with him wherever he went. What Lamonte liked best was taking photos of pretty girls around Los Angeles—actresses, singers, models, and beauty pageant winners—and selling them to *Jet* magazine, a *Reader's Digest*-sized weekly magazine filled with features and photos of interest to black audiences. Tough work, but someone had to do it.

His brother Donald—whose family nickname was "Duck"—told me that Lamonte was also shooting publicity shots for Motown's West Coast office in LA. "Maybe Lamonte can introduce you to the guys he knows at Motown," Duck said encouragingly.

Motown Records! They were the biggest thing happening for black artists. The "Motown sound" was all over the radio—the Supremes, the Four Tops, Smokey Robinson and the Miracles, and the Temptations, just to name a few. Berry Gordy Jr. founded Motown Records in Detroit in 1959, getting its name from "Motor City." He was helping so many black artists cross over from the R&B charts (where black artists were) to the pop music charts (where white listeners were) that Gordy opened a second office in Los Angeles.

I called Lamonte, and he said, sure, he'd love to introduce me to the Motown guys. When he mentioned that he was in real tight with Marc Gordon, the president of Motown's LA office, I asked him, "Can you get me in to see him?"

"Sure, Billy, but can you sing?" I could tell that Lamonte was covering his bases.

"Don't worry about that. Just get me into his office, and I'll do the rest."

Duck had planned a trip home to St. Louis, so I hitched a ride with him back to Los Angeles. The night before we left, I put my guitar and amp in the backseat and went drinking in a bar. When we came out at two in the morning, someone had stolen the instrument and amplifier. I was royally ticked off: How was I going to support myself while waiting for my break with Motown Records if I didn't have a guitar and an amp?

With St. Louis in our rearview mirror, Duck and I set out on Route 66 for the Golden State. I had one suitcase of clothes, $300 in my pocket, and a million stars in my eyes.

I loved Southern California upon arrival. Lamonte was glad to see me, and he seemed to know *everybody*. I could tell he had an eye for the ladies; he confided that he liked only two types of girls—"foreign and domestic." There was one who was especially beautiful, he said. He had taken pictures of her at a talent show for Miss Bronze California, and just like me, she wanted to become a singer too.

"What's her name?" I asked.

"Marilyn."

"One of the things Daddy liked

to do was gather my mother,

my sisters, and me around the

piano in our home and sing."

CHAPTER 3

CALIFORNIA SOUL

They say the sun comes up every morning . . .

Marilyn: Like Billy, I grew up knowing that I wanted to be a singer. I think I inherited that desire from my father because singing was his passion. When I was a baby and crying in my crib, Daddy would come in singing my name—*Mar-i-lyn*. That must have captivated me because my parents said I always stopped crying after Daddy sang to me. He proudly told everyone how well I responded to music.

By the time I was born, my father was no longer a professional singer but a physician and surgeon married to another doctor in general practice. Wayman McCoo met my mother, Mary Ellen Holloway, while they were both attending Meharry Medical College in Nashville, Tennessee, in the mid-1930s. At the time, and it's still true today, Meharry was the largest private, comprehensive black institution for educating health professionals and scientists in the United States.

Since my father was an only child and his father was a doctor, he was expected to follow in his father's footsteps. Daddy was amenable to that plan, but he also wanted to sing, so his father agreed to let him join a trio called the Jones Boys for a couple of years between college and medical school. They toured with Fletcher Henderson and his orchestra across the country.

Daddy knew he could only put medical school off for so long. Shortly after enrolling at Meharry Medical College, he met his future wife, Mary. They fell in love and were married in 1937. Following their internships, they settled in Columbus, Georgia, and opened a practice together, sharing office hours. Four children arrived over a seven-year period: I was born September 30, 1943, the second of four children. I had an older sister, Glenda, and two younger siblings, Millie and Wayman Jr.

Schools were segregated in the Deep South in the late 1940s, and the "separate but equal" public schools for black children were horrible. Among their other duties, my parents were the doctors for an all-black Catholic school in Phoenix City, Alabama, just a few miles away from Columbus across the Chattahoochee River. When they saw firsthand how black children received a better education from the nuns (who were white), they enrolled Glenda and me in that school, even though our family didn't attend a Catholic church. The nuns knew how to teach the three Rs, and they maintained classroom discipline with a wooden yardstick across your knuckles.

Mommy, who was raised in New Jersey, had difficulty dealing with the prevailing racial attitudes prevalent throughout the South. She was the Rosa Parks of her day, someone who wouldn't give up her seat on the bus for a white male, for instance. When she was treated with disrespect, she wasn't reluctant to speak up in her defense. My father used to say, "Mary, you're going to get us killed someday."

Back then, black children weren't allowed to try on shoes in shoe stores. My mother had to order shoes from a catalog, which deeply bothered her, and when the delivery people arrived on her doorstep, she never knew how she would be treated. One time, a white delivery boy knocked on the door. When she opened it, he rudely said, "Here you go, girl," and tossed the package of shoes at her feet. She promptly slammed the door in his face.

He pounded his fists on the door because he hadn't been paid yet for the COD package. Mommy opened the door and tossed the paper money and the coins into the front garden. "You're crazy, woman," the boy said, as he scrambled to pick up the loose change in the dirt.

I have to explain the mentality of the times. A black woman unafraid to give a white man a piece of her mind had to be "crazy" in a white person's eyes. And if she were crazy enough to say something, she must be the girlfriend of someone important—like the police chief or the mayor.

My father was always coming home to an adventure, never knowing what he would find, but he knew his Northern-raised bride and "good ol' boys" weren't a good fit. Since they were a well-educated, upwardly mobile couple with four children under the age of ten, they began to explore their options. They took a trip to Denver and Los Angeles to scout out a place to move the family. Los Angeles won out. In 1950, we packed up our belongings and joined the western migration.

Los Angeles was booming in the post–World War II years, but back in 1950, the city had about half as many people as today. My parents purchased a home on 10th Avenue between Adams Boulevard and 25th Street, a nice residential area that was integrated. I attended an integrated elementary school, my first experience with white children. The only white kids I knew back in Columbus were the ones I got into rock fights with. I found some of my new classmates to be very nice, and I made good friends of all colors. My closest friend in elementary school was a Japanese-American girl who lived across the street.

One of the things Daddy liked to do was gather my mother, my sisters, and me around the piano in our home and sing. Glenda and I were taking piano lessons, so he'd have one of us play while he taught us four-part harmonies. I loved the challenge of learning my part and singing it in the right key. My parents marveled at my ability to sing in the correct pitch and timbre, but I didn't understand what was so unusual about that. When Daddy asked me to sing a stanza at a certain intonation—he sounded a note on the piano as my cue—I sang correctly. At an early age, my ears were being trained to hear harmonies.

My parents made sure that we were exposed to various cultural events. They accompanied us whenever famous black singers or pianists came into town, took us to musicals, and exposed us to recitals. One time when I was young, they took us to see a famous Russian ballerina named Mia Slavenska, and for months afterward I wanted to become a ballerina in the worst way, but that ended when I saw a movie called *The Red Shoes*. The film was based on a story by Hans Christian Andersen about a young girl who buys a pair of enchanted red shoes to help her dance: The girl dances the night away but finds she cannot stop dancing or take off the shoes. Eventually, she dances herself to death, so I knew I didn't want to become a ballerina. Besides, with Daddy's encouragement, my heart's desire was to become a singer one day.

My parents belonged to the Medical, Dental, and Pharmaceutical Association, which consisted of black doctors, dentists, and pharmacists. Each year, the Los Angeles chapter put on a musical production and sold tickets to their patients and customers as a fundraiser toward scholarships for aspiring doctors, dentists, and pharmacists.

Like the von Trapp family who enthralled audiences in *The Sound of Music*, the McCoo family also sang in public. Daddy loved organizing the show each year for the Medical, Dental, and Pharmaceutical Association and teaching us our songs. When I was around thirteen years old, he insisted that I sing my first solo. I'll never forget when the lights were turned down, and I was bathed in the glow of a spotlight. For weeks, I had goose bumps just thinking about it.

Religion was not important to my parents. One of the few times I remember going to church at a young age was when we visited my grandparents on my father's side. They lived in Alabama, where Daddy grew up, and they usually took us to some holy-roller church where the preacher worked himself up into a lather while he preached the gospel. This one pastor would get pretty loud, so loud that Glenda and I would giggle at the most inopportune moments. My mother would cast an eye toward us that said, *You two cut it out. We're in church.*

As I entered high school, I told Mommy I was ready to try the Catholic church again. I think I was remembering Mother Mary Mission Catholic School back in Phoenix City. I liked the "high church" for all the wrong reasons—the drama, the genuflecting, making the sign of the cross, and the smell of incense.

I gave serious thought to getting baptized and becoming a Catholic, making it all official. I attended a class called "Religious Instruction" and heard the priest make what I considered a provocative statement: Human beings were the only members of God's creation who could think.

This didn't make sense to me. I raised my hand. "What about dogs when they run to a fence? If the dog sees the fence is low, he jumps over it. If he sees that it's too high, he burrows a hole under the fence. Either way, the dog is doing something to get around that fence."

The priest rebuffed me. "That's instinct, pure and simple," he said, moving on to other subjects. I approached him after the class, but he dismissed me, saying I needed to accept some things on faith. That troubled me, and not long thereafter, I lost interest in the Catholic church and things relating to God.

But I hadn't lost interest in singing. I loved to sing before anyone who would listen. If you came over to my parents' house when I was in elementary or junior high school, I would have insisted that you listen to me sing a song or two. I loved performing and the attention it brought me. Every time there was a talent show at school, I was the first to enter, and I loved singing big ballads and torch songs that displayed my range, classics like "The Man That Got Away," "The Nearness of You," or "That's All."

My father, seeing how much his daughter loved what *he* loved, said if I really wanted to sing, then I needed to study voice. I remember him saying that it bothered him whenever he heard black singers taking part in classical operas or serious musicals. "Their voices cloud up before the performance is over," he said. "Their problem is that their voices aren't strong because they haven't been properly trained. You need that training, which is why I think you should take voice lessons." My voice lessons began when I was thirteen.

I started my high school years at Los Angeles High on Olympic Boulevard, but during my junior year, we moved from 10th Avenue to View Park, an area that had been all white but was opening up to black families in the late 1950s. Our family encountered some interesting experiences integrating the area.

One time, a girlfriend and I were walking home from school (she was black too). A carload of white boys drove by, and they yelled out, "Niggers!" Gail looked up and said, "Hey, that's Scott from my biology class."

I told my mother and my father about the incident at dinner that night. Mommy wrote Mr. Toomey, the boys' vice principal at Dorsey High, explaining in no uncertain terms that she did not want her daughter harassed anymore, and if he couldn't control the behavior of the boys who attended his school, then she was going to call the police.

A couple of days later, I was requested to see Mr. Toomey in his office. While I sat outside waiting to see him, I could hear him chewing out Scott and his friends. "How could you say that?" he bellowed. "Don't you know that her mother is a *doctor?*"

I sat there feeling very unimpressed. Suppose my mother had been a maid? Would Scott and his friends have been called on the carpet then? Was it only wrong if my mother was a doctor?

Dorsey High was predominantly white when I attended school, where I was part of the class of 1960. On my first day on campus, I found out that they had scheduled a talent show, which was right up my alley. Naturally, I wanted to try out, but I needed a pianist to accompany me. Someone said there was a brilliant student named Marty Katz who was a prodigy with the piano. I found him in the choir room during lunch and introduced myself. "I want to audition for the talent show. Can you play the piano for me?" I inquired.

Marty was a friendly guy, and he warmed to the request. We agreed on a song we both knew, and when I finished singing the song for him, he thought I was absolutely wonderful. Just before lunch period was over, Mr. Rudy Saltzer, the choir director, walked into the choir room.

"Mr. Saltzer, you have to hear this young lady sing," said Marty.

So I sang my song again, and afterward, Mr. Saltzer asked to see my schedule of classes. I had a copy with me, and when I handed it to him, he said, "I'm changing your first period to choir."

I didn't have the heart to tell Mr. Saltzer that I didn't want to be in choir. Because of his enthusiasm, though, I thought I would give it a try. I'm glad I did because he taught me the importance of discipline and commitment.

I also took drama classes at Dorsey High, and I was the first black student to be cast in a lead role when I played Countess Aurelia in *The Madwoman of Chaillot*. People said nice things about my singing and acting abilities, which prompted me to think about not going to college so I could pursue a singing career. My voice coach, Eddie Beal, believed I had the talent to go somewhere—and that somewhere was singing popular music. That was what I wanted to hear because I dreamed of singing and acting like Judy Garland, who was called the "world's greatest entertainer" in the 1960s.

I graduated from Dorsey High when I was sixteen because I started a year early back at Mother Mary Mission. As I discussed my future with my parents, we both concluded that I was a bit young to throw all my eggs into the singing career basket, so we agreed that I should attend college. I had been admitted to UCLA, just a half-hour drive away from home. I could live at home and continue pursuing my music.

When I arrived on campus, I immediately declared myself as a music major. Meanwhile, I began taking vocal lessons off campus with an awesome teacher named Florence Russell, whom my father and Eddie Beal found. Mrs. Russell improved my voice's upper range and taught me arias and other classical songs. I didn't see myself becoming classically trained since I wanted to sing popular music, but I realized the training would be good for me.

Since I was receiving so much musical training from Mrs. Russell, I changed my major to theater arts—drama. I must confess, though, that I felt like just another student on the large UCLA campus in west Los Angeles, and I wondered why I was there. I figured I would get by until something broke in my music career.

One of the things I did was join a jazz ensemble. One of the guys in the group was Lamonte McLemore, an interesting character who always seemed to have a camera in his hands. The group leader was Rex Middleton, who taught us various jazz arrangements to sing. I loved singing in harmony because it reminded me of times when my father gathered our family around the piano and taught us four-part harmonies.

We initially called our little jazz group the Hi-Fi's, a play on "high-fidelity," which was how records sounded before the introduction of stereo recordings. During my junior year at UCLA, we received a wonderful opportunity: Ray Charles wanted us to open for him on a three-week tour. This was in the middle of the spring semester, however, which was bad timing for me since I was the only group member still in school.

I thoroughly enjoyed my time on the road, although I ended up on academic probation at UCLA for my three-week disappearing act. Touring and singing in front of audiences was everything I thought it would be. I could see this lifestyle working for me, so when the opportunity came for the Hi-Fi's to open for Ray Charles the following fall, I dropped out of UCLA for the semester, vowing to my mother—with fingers crossed behind my back—that I would finish upon my return three months later.

Three months on the road with Ray Charles and the Raelettes were an eye-opener. First, I saw how hard everyone worked—flying and driving to the next stop, setting up, performing the show, and packing up for the next town. I felt that the Raelettes—four young women singing backup to Ray's gritty vocals—were disrespected by the musicians and road crew. They were sometimes cussed out and treated rudely. I felt sorry for the Raelettes, who probably figured they would be replaced if they complained about their treatment. That helped me decide to make good on my promise to my mother to go back to school and get my degree.

Education was important in our home, which is why I changed my major from theater arts to business administration before my junior year.

All the theater arts majors I met were selling tickets and ushering in theaters after they graduated. Despite the success of some black actresses, including Ruby Dee and Diahann Carroll, deep down I wondered how many other opportunities there would be for other young, ambitious black actresses. At least a business major had greater job prospects to fall back on, I thought.

In spite of some of the negative things I saw on the road, the fall tour in 1964 confirmed my growing desire to make singing my career. I was serious about making that happen, but I began having problems with our jazz group—which we had renamed the Vocals prior to touring with Ray Charles—following our return from the tour. For instance, we would set a rehearsal time at one o'clock in the afternoon. I would bust my hump to get there on time, juggling my classes and homework assignments. Then I would sit around for a couple hours while the guys straggled in. That got old, and my patience wore thin.

The Vocals broke up as 1964 drew to a close, which I expected. I returned to UCLA, feeling unsettled in my life. I wasn't sure where my music career was heading, and my parents' marriage, which had been in trouble for years, was breaking up. Daddy had been absent from home for long stretches, and then he started missing holidays. That hurt me because we had this music connection between us, and his rejection of Mommy felt like a rejection of my siblings and me. I struggled with feelings of anger and disappointment.

One weekend, I attended a concert at the Coconut Grove with some friends that changed my life. Johnny Mathis was performing that night, but I was the one who was nervous. As Johnny crooned some big hits with his sweet-sounding voice, I became more frustrated. Not with Johnny, but with myself, because I *loved* how he was performing, and that was what *I* wanted to do. *I have to do this*, I decided. *I don't know how, but I have to do this.*

I was coming to understand how strong this desire was to sing and perform, and it wasn't going to disappear. First, though, I had to graduate from college. I owed that to my parents. Since I missed the entire fall semester because I was out on the road with Ray Charles, I took double sessions during the summer of 1965 and graduated with a degree in business administration. I took a job in Century City as an executive trainee with Joseph Magnin, a high-end department store, while I continued to live at home.

Although the Vocals were history as far as singing together, I still hung out on weekends with several group members. One Saturday night I found myself at Lamonte's apartment—which we called "Hobo Flats"—where I was introduced to a friend of Lamonte's who had come out from St. Louis.

"Marilyn, meet my friend Billy Davis, Jr., but back home in St. Looie, they call him June Bug. Isn't that right, Bugs?"

This Billy Davis character chuckled. I had heard about him from the guys. He had this thousand-watt smile and quick laugh that filled the room. I noticed his hair had been "processed" real straight and real slick, just like the popular singers of the day.

"Yeah, Billy can really sing," Lamonte said. "He's out here trying to get a deal with Motown."

"Really?" I said, more than a bit intrigued. "How's that going?"

"Well, through Lamonte, I met with Marc Gordon, the president of Motown Records out here in LA, which led to an audition," Billy replied. "The Motown folks said they liked me very much, but the best they could do was put me on the waiting list."

"What's the waiting list?" I asked, wondering if it were something more than being on, well, a waiting list.

"Let me explain," Billy said. "Everybody wants to be with Motown. They're the label with a ton of hits. What they do is take young, talented singers into the studio and produce their demos. These demos are then shipped back to Motown's home offices in Detroit, and every Friday morning a committee listens to these demos, asking themselves if there are any hits in the bunch. What they don't tell you is that you're in there against the Supremes, the Temptations, and the Four Tops. How can you compete against that?"

I shook my head in disbelief. The task sounded daunting.

"If they hear something they like, they take you into the studio and start all over. Then they send your record back to Detroit for another listen. If they like it this time around, they do everything they can to make it a hit. If they don't hear a hit, they may send you back into the studio and cut some more songs."

"And you think you can make it," I said.

"That's what I want to do," he replied cheerfully. "As far as I'm concerned, being on the waiting list is just another step closer."

Billy was funny and fun to be around, the life-of-a-party type who always seemed to have a drink in his hand. I could tell that he was passionate about music. After a couple of hours of conversing, I learned that Billy, who was five years older than I was, had more life experiences in his little pinky than I had on two hands. After dropping out of high school, he had worked a variety of jobs, sung with different groups, been stationed in Europe with the US army, and even owned a nightclub in St. Louis. On the personal front, he said he was separated from his wife, but a divorce was in the offing.

A couple of months passed by, and through Lamonte and Billy, I met a Motown producer named Hal Davis. He agreed to take me into the studio to cut a couple of demos, but nothing ever happened after they were shipped back to Detroit for the Friday morning listen. When I inquired about my status, I was told that I, too, was put on the infamous Motown "waiting list."

In the fall of 1965, Billy was living with Lamonte and his brother Duck, and while Lamonte had his freelance photography for *Jet* magazine's "Beauty of the Week" feature to fall back on, Billy was looking for something to do while he waited for Motown to pluck him out of obscurity.

"Why don't we try some group singing?" Lamonte said to Billy one day, remembering the fun he had had with the Hi-Fi's.

"That sounds like an idea," Billy said. "I've always liked singing in groups."

"We need some girls to join us," Lamonte said. "I know what we'll do. We'll call Marilyn and the other girl who used to sing with us, Fritzi. They aren't doing anything."

"Just so you know," Billy said, "I'm not giving up on my solo career."

"No, it'll be something to do until Motown picks you up."

Before Lamonte could call me, however, a fellow named Ronald Townson dropped by their place. Lamonte knew Ronald from St. Louis, where they had attended the same high school together. Like Billy, Ronald had been singing since childhood and was well-versed in opera and an experienced choir director. When he moved to Los Angeles in 1957, Ronald had come out West on a star search as well, and he was still searching. Ronald had a smile and a laugh that were contagious, and a big heart as well. He had married his childhood sweetheart, Bobette, gotten a job as a postman, and witnessed the arrival of two children. When Lamonte asked him about joining their little group effort, Ronald said that sounded fine.

Up, Up and Away

Singing in a group *didn't* sound fine to me when Lamonte sounded me out. "You remember how nobody was serious about it when we were doing the Hi-Fi's," I reminded him. "I've had enough of picking up people from their girlfriend's house and starting rehearsals two hours late."

When Lamonte found out his idea wasn't sitting well with me, he handed the phone over to Billy. "No, this will be different," Billy began. "First of all, we're talking about doing this as a hobby—something to pass the time until our solo careers get going. And I think we are all professional enough to show up on time for practice. We'll rehearse after you get off work."

I asked Billy who else would sing with us. "Lamonte thinks we should ask Fritzi. I don't know her, but you do, of course. We've asked a guy named Ronald Townson to join us." I knew Ronald from the beginning days of the Hi-Fi's. He had been in the group for a couple of months.

When Lamonte and Billy called Fritzi, however, she had something else going. Her interests were leading her elsewhere.

"We have to find another girl to take Fritzi's place," Lamonte said. "Hey, I know who we can call—Florence LaRue. I took her photo at the Miss Bronze California Beauty Pageant."

"Really?" I said. "What a coincidence," I deadpanned. It was a long-running joke that Lamonte had photographed more beautiful black women than anyone.

I knew of Florence. I had entered the Miss Bronze California pageant in 1962, which gave out awards in several categories: beauty, talent, and congeniality. I entered the contest, thinking that if I won the Grand Talent award, a record executive in the audience would notice and sign me to a record deal. My interest wasn't in the beauty portion of the contest. I knew I didn't have the body to win because I believed my legs were bowed and much too thin. For the Grand Talent competition, I sang "Our Love Is Here to Stay", made famous by Nat King Cole, with Eddie Beal on the piano. Following my winning performance, Lamonte snapped my picture for *Jet* magazine.

When the Miss Bronze California pageant came around the following year, I was singing in the Hi-Fi's with Lamonte. Thanks to his connections, he arranged it so the Hi-Fi's could sing as part of the Miss Bronze California's entertainment while the judges were voting who would win.

During the Grand Talent award competition, I watched Florence sing "April in Paris" in French ("Avril en Paris"), which brought the house down. When she learned that she had won the Grand Talent Award, she, too, had her picture taken by Lamonte for *Jet* magazine. So when Lamonte asked me about Florence joining the group, I knew she could sing. Lamonte made the call, and Florence, a schoolteacher at Grant Elementary School in Hollywood, said she'd love to sing with us.

The five of us started rehearsing, and what we were producing started to sound pretty good. You know, when singers sing, they want to show off their stuff, and we soon began talking about how we could do just that.

We needed a name. Suggestions were thrown out, and the one we liked the best was "The Versatiles." It seemed to fit since we had so many types of voices. We were *versatile*. Get it?

I think the first time we sang in public was at the Adams West, an old theater on Adams Boulevard. The Adams West had become an after-hours place that featured acts trying to break into the music business. We also performed at a billiard parlor—a glorified pool hall—called Dick Griffey's Guys & Dolls. Everyone had fun being on a stage—even if the stage overlooked heavyset guys shooting eight ball in the back.

Lamonte, who was the one organizing things, found us another gig at Maverick's Flat, owned by John Daniels, which happened to be a real hangout in the mid-Sixties. Little did I know that Lamonte had another plan going.

"Lamonte, I told you—

when I sign with a label,

it will be for myself.

I don't want to

sing in a group."

CHAPTER 4

GoWHERE YOU WANNA GO

You gotta go where you wanna go,
do what you wanna do . . .

Billy: That Lamonte was a sneaky guy. He had this day job taking publicity photos of the new up-and-coming acts at Motown Records West Coast office, but he kept whispering into Marc Gordon's ear that he really needed to hear the Versatiles sing because we were an act he'd want to sign up.

Marc sent a couple of his A&R guys out to catch us at venues like Adams West. A&R stands for "artist and repertoire," and they are responsible for scouting new talent and getting them signed. But we never received a phone call saying that Marc wanted to meet with us.

Meanwhile, Lamonte was also working all the angles. Since I was on the Motown waiting list, Lamonte said that I should approach Marc Gordon and see whether he wanted to sign up the Versatiles. I kept saying, "Lamonte, I told you—when I sign with a label, it will be for myself. I don't want to sing in a group."

"Yeah, but what can it hurt?" Lamonte replied.

Marilyn: I was echoing what Billy was saying because I still saw the Versatiles as a diversion until someone realized that I was the next Judy Garland. But Lamonte insisted that if Motown signed us as a group, then that would be a great way for me to pursue a solo career because then I would have my go-go boot in the door with Motown.

Lamonte has the gift of gab, and half of what he was saying made sense, so we went along with it, figuring, *Let's not be stupid about the whole thing.* We submitted a demo produced by one of Motown's aspiring producers, Hal Davis (no relation to Billy), but it was rejected at one of those famous Friday morning listening sessions back in Detroit.

When Marc finally got around to catching our act, we hoped that a strong recommendation from him would get us a second look by the Motown powers in Detroit. But that never happened, and then Marc abruptly decided to leave Motown to pursue other ventures in the recording and entertainment business.

One of our few contacts was gone. What do we do now? We continued to rehearse several nights a week and sing in small clubs for tip change. Then Lamonte received an interesting phone call from Marc, who said he was officially in the management business. The first act he was interested in managing was . . . us!

Billy: Marc said, "I believe in you guys. I think you have the talent, and I would love to manage you." We were like, *Wow, someone wants to manage our group.*

I had mixed feelings, however. I felt like I was getting sucked into this group thing, yet I still wanted a solo career. Marc knew the business, though, and if he thought the Versatiles had a chance to make it, then that couldn't be a bad thing. Besides, a solo career with Motown wasn't looking too promising. I had been on the waiting list for the better part of a year, and nothing had happened. The fact that Marc thought he could find us a label sounded pretty good to these ears.

Marilyn: So our solo aspirations took a backseat when Marc became our manager. He rolled up his sleeves and quickly found us a record deal with a small label called Bronco Records in the summer of 1966.

Oh, well, it wasn't Motown, but at least it was a start. Bronco rushed us into a rented studio and had us record "You're Good Enough for Me." The record received some radio airplay in Los Angeles, but it quickly disappeared from sight.

Marc, meanwhile, was beating the bushes for a better record label. He struck up a friendship with Johnny Rivers, who had become a very successful recording artist in his own right. He was credited with contributing to the start of the American discotheque craze at the Whisky A-Go-Go in Los Angeles in 1963. One of his big hit singles, "Secret Agent Man," was the theme song of a hit TV show at the time.

Because of his success, Liberty Records had given him a deal to start his own record label. This was something very new back then, but Johnny was a smart businessman—and young, since he was in his mid-twenties. Johnny loved R&B, and he expressed a strong interest in coproducing some acts with Marc on his new Soul City Records label. The first act Marc proposed was the Versatiles. Johnny checked us out, liked what he saw, and signed us as his first act. This happened in the fall of 1966.

Naturally, the group was thrilled with this development. We were invited to show up at the Liberty Records studio on Sunset Boulevard, where Johnny listened to us rehearse one evening. When we were finished,

Johnny called us over to his soundboard. "I think you have a great chance to make it," he said, "but your name has got to go."

"You mean the Versatiles?" Billy asked. "What is it you don't like about it?"

"It has an old sound to it. It's not hip enough."

We didn't mind hearing that Johnny thought we needed to change the group's name. I don't think anyone in the group was married to "The Versatiles." We huddled around Marc's desk to discuss the situation, and we left that meeting with an assignment—come back the next day with ideas for a new name. As I drove Billy back to his apartment (he still didn't have a car), we tossed out names. I liked the name "Mark V" (as in "Mark Five"), which was a play off of the Lincoln Mark III, a popular luxury car at the time. I also liked the way "Mark V" tied in with our manager's name because I thought so highly of Marc Gordon.

When Billy heard me tout the "Mark V," however, he grimaced.

"Why don't you like my name?" I pouted.

"It . . . it doesn't sound like a music group. It sounds like a Lincoln," he offered.

But he didn't have anything better.

When Ronald went home that night, he told his wife, Bobette, that Johnny Rivers said we needed a new name. They began tossing names into the air as well.

"How about the Third Dimension?" Ronald offered.

Bobette was intrigued. "Third Dimension? What do you mean?"

"You know, 3-D and all that. The third dimension refers to depth, like how a solid object differs from a two-dimensional drawing of it."

They kicked that concept around some more. Bobette said she remembered something about the fourth dimension being about time, and the fifth dimension—

"—is about sound!" Ronald exclaimed. "That's it—we'll call ourselves the Fifth Dimension. We're five in the group, right?"

We came back the next day, and everyone shared the names they came up with, and by far the "Fifth Dimension" was the clear-cut winner. When someone said the fifth dimension could be about sound, we liked that idea. We decided to use the numeral instead of spelling it out. Marc and Johnny made it unanimous when we presented the name change to them.

The "5th Dimension" certainly fit with the times. Rod Serling, the creator of *The Twilight Zone*, a popular TV show in the 1960s, started his creepy show by intoning, "There is a fifth dimension beyond that which is known to man. It is a dimension as vast as space and timeless as infinity. It is the middle ground between light and shadow, between science and superstition, and it lies between the pits of man's fears and the summit of his knowledge. This is the dimension of imagination. It is an area which we call . . . The Twilight Zone."

Hey, we weren't that deep. We were five singers, right? From that day forward, we were officially known as the 5th Dimension. The publicity people at Soul City Records cranked out a press release announcing the name change, calling our quintet a "new dimension in sound, a convergence of the 1960s that explodes the mold from which groups are formed."

I know, you had to be there, but that's how many people felt in the Sixties. This was the time when phrases like "revolutionary," "free love," "psychedelic," and "power to the people" were being thrown around like cheap Frisbees. Understand the mood of the times: The country had undergone a massive upheaval following the assassination of President Kennedy in 1963, and President Johnson was "escalating" the Vietnam

War by pouring hundreds of thousands of American troops into Southeast Asia. Protest marches were picking up on college campuses, guys were growing their hair long, girls were wearing miniskirts, and protest marchers were talking about "making love, not war."

Billy: Another friend of Lamonte's was brought in to help us with our stage presentation and put some more polish into our act. An arranger named René DeKnight, who would double as the group's musical director for the next few years, began helping us produce the right sound and make the right moves on stage. René was also an accomplished pianist, and he played with the Delta Rhythm Boys for a number of years dating back to the 1940s, so he knew how to stage a show. He would become our keyboardist during our live performances.

Meanwhile, Johnny heard that our first single with Bronco Records bombed, so he knew how important our first single with Soul City Records would be. He decided that a song called "I'll Be Lovin' You Forever" by Willie Hutch would be a good fit for this new group with a "contemporary" sound. I sang the lead on "I'll Be Lovin' You Forever," which had a Four Tops feel to it. While our effort received good airplay in Los Angeles, the song never gained any traction outside Southern California. Our second single had bitten the dust rather quickly.

Now we were oh-for-two, and I wouldn't say that we were down to our last swing, but we were certainly behind in the count.

We needed a hit—bad.

Marilyn: Nothing establishes a group more than having a hit. Johnny Rivers studied our situation, and he said we needed to follow the example of Elvis, the Beatles, and the Rolling Stones by "covering" another artist's song and trying to get some radio play.

Remember, the pop music industry was in its infancy in the 1950s and early 1960s, and the way to make it in those days was to get something on the charts—the Billboard Top 40. The charts were made up of "singles" released on 45 rpm records—seven-inch records that had an A side (the single) and a B side (a filler song). If your single received airplay on radio stations (based on audience requests and other factors), this created sales for your single, which moved you up the charts. People who bought your single often purchased your album, which created more sales and—potentially—the release of more "singles" off the album.

So, how do you go about making that first hit single? The safest and most secure route for everyone—from the record label to the DJ "spinning the platters" in the booth—was to record your version of another musician's song. This was known in the industry as a "cover."

Covers were done all the time in those days. Half the songs on the Beatles' debut album, *Please, Please Me*, were covers. "Twist and Shout," a big hit in 1963, was a cover of a Bert Russell/Phil Medley composition performed by the Isley Brothers a year earlier. The Rolling Stones' first single in 1963 was Chuck Berry's "Come on Over," and the Stones followed that up by releasing "I Wanna Be Your Man"—a Beatles song written by John Lennon and Paul McCartney!

This was the mind-set of the industry as we hunted for a song to be our first hit single. Johnny suggested covering "Go Where You Wanna Go," written by John Phillips of the Mamas and Papas and released on their album but never as a single. Johnny said this upbeat pop tune would be an excellent match for what we were trying to do with our new group.

The lyrics certainly matched the "free love" of the hippie era:

You gotta go where you wanna go
Do what you wanna do
With whoever you wanna do it babe

You don't understand
That a girl like me can love just one man
Three thousand miles, that's how far you'll go
And you said to me "Please don't follow"

Billy: I don't think anyone would ever call "Go Where You Wanna Go" a song with soul. Initially I was worried that it was too pop, but like I said, we needed a hit. So we went into the studio and gave it our best shot.

Johnny was right. "Go Where You Wanna Go" went straight up the pop charts because we did not have a "black" sound. I doubt that one in ten disc jockeys thought that the 5th Dimension was a group of black singers. Back in those days, practically all black singers had to start on the R&B charts, which was music played by black DJs on black radio stations. Music was more segregated than you would think back then. After black artists earned their chops on the R&B charts, *then* they were given the opportunity to cross over onto the pop charts. Everyone—black or white—wanted to make it on the pop circuit because that meant you were selling more records and making more money. You were mainstream.

What Motown did was establish a route for black artists to easily cross over. Proven acts like the Supremes, the Temptations, and the Four Tops had an easier time crossing over to the pop charts and didn't have to worry about getting to a certain place on the R&B charts.

This was the ocean we were swimming in when "Go Where You Wanna Go" debuted on the charts on January 14, 1967. I'll never forget the first time I heard us on the radio. I nearly drove the car off the road because I was so excited.

We called my family back in St. Louis and told them they *had* to call the local radio stations and ask them to play it, so I'm sure it was a hit in that market. In Los Angeles, we took turns telephoning KHJ, home of "Boss Radio" and the biggest AM station playing the hits, to request "Go Where You Wanna Go."

I'd call up and say, "Hello? KHJ? Yes, I want to hear that song by that group—what's their name? The 5th Estate? I think their song is called 'Go Where You Wanna Go.'"

Marilyn: We broke into the Top Twenty nationally, reaching No. 16 on the charts. Now we felt like we had some momentum going. The plans called for releasing our first album, so Johnny hired a young talented songwriter to help us out—an earnest twenty-year-old named Jimmy Webb. He came highly recommended from Marc Gordon, who worked with him at Motown.

Jimmy, a minister's son, grew up in Oklahoma playing the organ in his father's church. What he liked doing was rearranging and reharmonizing hymns and coming up with a fresh approach to old melodies. Knowing that he wanted to become a songwriter, he came out West following high school and enrolled at San Bernardino Valley College, where he was a music student. He pounded on some doors in Hollywood, and the story goes that a young Jimmy and a white, blond backup band marched into the offices of Motown Records in Los Angeles looking for work, which took some nerve. Even though a white kid and Motown Records weren't a good match at the time, he did make a lasting impression on Marc Gordon. A few months later, when Marc's position was axed, he thought enough of Jimmy's enthusiasm and talents to introduce him to Johnny Rivers.

Johnny liked what he heard and hired him on the spot, signing him to a contract. Jimmy's first assignment was to work with us on our debut album. The first time we met in the studio with Jimmy, we found him in a corner fooling around on the piano.

"Come on over," he said in his friendly Oklahoma twang, "and you can listen to what I'm working on." He told us he had recently spent a week-end in San Bernardino with a friend at KMEN radio. The radio station was using a hot air balloon to promote KMEN, and Jimmy took his first ride in one. Jimmy was enamored with the colorful hot air balloons, and he and his friend talked about doing a film one day about them. "I've got this great idea for a film title," said his friend.

"What would that be?" Jimmy asked.

"*Up, Up and Away.*"

Jimmy said something clicked for him when he heard the words "Up, Up and Away." He snuck into a practice room at San Bernardino Valley College and began playing a tune that came into his head. A few bars here, a stanza there, and he had a song.

"Let me play it for you," he said, and when we heard the upbeat tempo of "Up, Up and Away," we loved it, but it sounded like an album cut to us because it was so pretty. We didn't believe "Up, Up and Away" could be a hit in the market at that time.

Jimmy arranged the song, and we worked on the vocals together. It was clear that he had a gift for strong, varied rhythms, inventive structures, and rich harmonies. This was also the first time we worked with a top-flight engineer named Bones Howe, and his specialty was recording our voices twice and "layering" our voices on top of each other. This gave our sound a richer, deeper resonance.

We recorded "Up, Up and Away" in late 1966 and made it the title song of our debut album. As Johnny and Marc debated which song we should release as a single, they felt that "Another Day, Another Heartache" would be a good follow-up to "Go Where You Wanna Go." They had no plans to release "Up, Up and Away" as a single because they shared our view that Jimmy Webb's song was nothing more than an album cut—a nice song that would never catch an audience on the Billboard Top 40.

When our *Up, Up and Away* album hit the streets, a fellow named Johnny Mann of the Johnny Mann Singers listened to the title cut. To his ears, "Up, Up and Away" sounded like a hit, so he immediately wanted to cover it.

As a professional courtesy, Johnny Mann called Johnny Rivers and asked him whether we had any plans to release "Up, Up and Away" as a single. Johnny said no. "Be my guest and cover it if you want," he told his colleague.

Johnny Mann said thank you very much and hung up the phone. Sensing an opening, he rushed into the studio, and his group, the Johnny Mann Singers, recorded "Up, Up and Away" and released it in May 1967.

The song received immediate attention and started climbing the charts like a, well, hot air balloon. This development certainly flashed on our radar screen, so we met with Marc and Johnny to discuss our options. Johnny felt that we were missing a chance for a hit. His advice was that we release our version of "Up, Up and Away" *tomorrow*.

That's what we did. I would say that for at least a month, *two* versions of "Up, Up and Away" fought for chart supremacy, dueling for a spot on the Top 40. We caught a big break when our version prevailed, which, in the grand scheme of things, was huge for us. Let's face it: "Up, Up and

Away" established the 5th Dimension, won us national acclaim, and kickstarted our career. We wouldn't be where we are today without "Up, Up and Away".

We are often asked why "Up, Up and Away" was such a big song. We think its optimistic tone caught the mood of the country at exactly the right time.

Would you like to ride in my beautiful balloon?
Would you like to glide in my beautiful balloon?
We could float among the stars together, you and I.

For we can fly.
We can fly!
Up, up and away, my beautiful, my beautiful balloon!

The song transported listeners to a more beautiful place, and Lord knows, the American public needed a lift in 1967. The Vietnam War was splitting the country apart, college campuses were paralyzed by sit-ins and demonstrations, and there was talk of revolution in the streets. Astronauts Gus Grissom, Ed White, and Roger Chaffee died on January 27, 1967, in the Apollo spacecraft flash fire during a launch pad test at Kennedy Space Center, Florida, dealing a severe blow in the race to put the first man on the moon. Closer to home, race riots in Detroit and Newark turned black neighborhoods into smoldering ruins during the summer of 1967. Our hit was the "don't worry, be happy" song of its time. You could be stuck in the middle of freeway traffic, but when you heard "Up, Up and Away," the song made you feel good and allowed you to forget whatever was happening in your life.

TWA Airlines wanted to use our recording of "Up, Up and Away" as part of a new ad campaign, but Marc Gordon told us they lowballed their offer, so we turned them down. TWA went out and found five singers to duplicate what we had done in the studio and used "Up, Up and Away" in their ad campaign anyway. We sued and lost in court, but you couldn't get away with that today. We'll tell you how big those TWA commercials became: When Barbra Streisand was introduced to Jimmy Webb, she asked him whether he was the guy who "made a hit song out of that commercial."

Although "Up, Up and Away" never reached No. 1, the song won five Grammys, including the jaw-dropping "Record of the Year." "Up, Up and Away" also won "Song of the Year," "Best Contemporary Single," "Best Performance by a Vocal Group," and "Best Contemporary Group Performance, Vocal or Instrumental." Too bad the Grammys weren't televised in those days and the red carpet was only three feet wide and thirty feet long!

"Up, Up and Away" turned the 5th Dimension into an overnight success. Like a flash of lightning across a summer sky, millions of Americans were humming *For we can fly! Up, up and a-waaaay* . . . Marc Gordon's desk stacked up with phone messages from promoters wanting to book us for concerts, fairs, and other engagements, and the daytime jobs and nighttime rehearsals became a distant memory.

The future looked as bright as a hot air balloon rising above the desert landscape. We were on our way to catching this thing called "success," and Billy and I were on our way to catching something equally mysterious—love.

"We became buddies

through those car rides

together, and I liked

his spirit and his heart."

CHAPTER 5

WORKIN' ON A GROOVY THING

I feel good when you are near,
I'm alive 'cause you are here . . .

Marilyn: In the months leading up to the release of "Up, Up and Away," Billy and his buddy Sonny Porter had rented an apartment on 60th Street not far from downtown LA Billy didn't have a car in those days, which sounds rather unbelievable for someone living in Southern California, but he seemed to have a million friends who could give him a ride whenever he needed to go somewhere.

One of those friends was me. We were rehearsing three or four nights a week at Marc Gordon's office on La Brea Avenue, and Billy needed a lift. I was glad to help out because my apartment was close to his, and we were headed in the same direction. I liked Billy, but not in any sort of romantic way. He struck me as a ladies' man who didn't lack for female attention. I found him to be a happy, fun-to-be-around guy who made me laugh, which helped pass the time whenever we sat in a traffic jam. We never lacked for topics to discuss—what it would be like performing live, improvements in our vocal phrasing, and whether this "group thing" would ever amount to anything.

We became buddies through those car rides together, and I liked his spirit and his heart. We rehearsed for several hours each evening, working on our stage show under the watchful eye of René DeKnight and blending our voices in sweet harmony. When we were done rehearsing, I would drive Billy to parties we were invited to, especially on the weekends.

Billy and I were spending more and more time hanging out together. I must confess, however, that I did not see him as boyfriend material. During one of our early rehearsals, I remember watching Billy sing, snapping his fingers and rocking with the beat. *What a shame he doesn't appeal to me,* I thought. Reason? The physical attraction was not there. He was shorter than the guys I was previously attracted to, but I found him to be muscular and built like a sparkplug. I was lean and tall for a woman at five-feet, eight-and-one-half inches—the same height as Billy. My pattern had been falling for someone taller and thin like me, so Billy definitely didn't match my physical type.

I'm better off this way, I thought. I heard that "relationships" in the entertainment business—especially the music field—weren't a good idea. These relationships never lasted, they said, so when the inevitable break-up arrived, two people who couldn't stand each other now had to sing *together.* The more I thought about it, I knew it would be better to remain good friends.

Billy: I can remember looking at Marilyn, too, and wondering if she was someone that I wanted to, you know, get to know better. I greatly appreciated her physical beauty, and she was built pretty good, but I didn't think she was my physical type either.

I wasn't thinking about anything more than friendship while we were forming the 5th Dimension. During those rides to rehearsals, we would just talk and talk—about the future of the group, if Motown would sign us, and things going on in the news. We discussed things that mattered. I could see that she had a good heart, and I was glad to have another friend. As for the boyfriend/girlfriend thing, though, I didn't see that happening.

Marilyn: Billy and I would talk about his relationships with girlfriends, and I would tell him about whom I was seeing on the side. We talked about guys who had one-track minds and the games they often played with women. He sympathized with me, adding that he wouldn't lie to a woman to get her to go to bed with him. "I don't believe in playing with a woman's feelings," he said.

I started to see Billy in a new light about the time "Up, Up and Away" was released in the late spring of 1967. One time, I was checking out an outfit Billy was wearing: a white satin shirt, blue-and-white plaid pants with the bell-bottoms, and white boots. His blue-and-white plaid pants caught my eye because they were snug and fit him well, and he also moved very well on stage. *Wow, Billy is kind of sexy.*

Billy's pants always seemed to be getting him into trouble. One time we were performing at Fairfax High School in Los Angeles during the early days. We were in the midst of performing "Shake Your Tambourine" when Billy performed a big dip and caused his pants to split. The seam on his right thigh opened up for the whole world to see.

We kept going like nothing had happened. When Billy, who was singing lead vocals, noticed that his pants had split, he smoothly turned sideways so that the audience couldn't see his exposed thigh. He stayed in that same awkward position for the rest of the concert, and it was all I could do to stop from busting up.

Something more serious happened when Marc Gordon called the group into his office for an important meeting. After going around the table and asking how everyone was doing, he announced that he believed it was time to quit our daytime jobs to rehearse more and travel to gigs now starting to come in across the country.

I wasn't sure how to take this suggestion. On the one hand, it was good news because Marc thought "Up, Up and Away" would be a hit and we would soon become very busy. On the other hand, it was bad news because that meant burning our bridges in the real world. Ronald couldn't continue delivering the mail, nor could Florence continue teaching kids at Grant Elementary. For the three of us with steady jobs, this was a step of faith.

My job was a well-paying one in Watts—also known as South-Central LA—working for a federal jobs program. Watts, a predominantly black suburb, had exploded in fury during the summer of 1965. Remember, this was during the civil rights era, and the previous year, 1964, marked a watershed moment in American history when President Lyndon Johnson signed the Civil Rights Act. But Californians acted to circumvent the law by passing Proposition 14, which invalidated the fair housing aspects of the Civil Rights Act. Feelings of injustice and despair were already smoldering in the inner city, and when the LAPD arrested a drunk driver in the summer of 1965, that provided the spark to light the fire of seething feelings. The Watts riots lasted six days, resulting in the deaths of thirty-four people, almost all black, and the destruction of hundreds of buildings and businesses, which burned to rubble.

As a response to the Watts riots, President Johnson pushed through his Great Society legislation, which included massive funding for what was called the War on Poverty. My job was to help people coming out of federal youth training and employment programs to find jobs. My $200 a week salary was good money—or "high cotton," as we had said in the South.

"How much money do you need to cover your bills?" Marc asked the group. We looked at each other and shrugged our shoulders.

"A hundred dollars a week," I said. I was raring to go, and I had kept my lifestyle lean and mean. I didn't mind taking a 50 percent pay cut to sing because this is what I wanted to do all my life.

"I don't think so," Ronald interjected. "I have a wife and two children to feed."

"I don't need much for myself," Billy said, "but I send money to St. Louis for my son."

Marc assured us that we would find enough work to allow us to cover our needs.

True to his word, Marc began booking us into clubs. One of our early gigs took us to Bimbo's 365 Club in San Francisco, a hallowed club that opened in 1951 near the hopping North Beach district. Bimbo's had a plush main room and an adjacent lounge. Florence and I shared a hotel room nearby, while the three guys holed up in a little hotel-apartment place called the Hyde Park Apartments. These were definitely budget accommodations to keep expenses down, but we didn't mind. Marc set up some interviews with several radio stations during our two-week engagement at Bimbo's.

For some reason, I cast a longer look at the guy in the blue-and-white plaid pants. One night after a show, Florence and I stopped at a nearby grocery and purchased some salami and Cold Duck—a cheap beverage made of sparkling Burgundy and champagne. The sweet fizzy concoction was popular in the Sixties.

"Let's invite Billy over," I heard myself saying to Florence.

"Good idea," she replied. "He'll make things fun."

We giggled like schoolgirls because we both knew that Billy was a teddy bear. When he knocked on the thin wooden door that night, however, my heart skipped a beat and my throat tightened. My attraction buttons had definitely been pushed, but I tried to be cool.

Billy: I can truthfully say, while I liked Marilyn's company in those early days, something in the back of my mind told me to be cool. I had been in show business longer than anyone in the group, so I remembered the old show business axiom that work and love don't mix, just as some people say you shouldn't have a relationship in the office where you work. I enjoyed eating salami and drinking Cold Duck—especially the latter activity—with Marilyn and Florence, and the three of us always had a good time together. But Marilyn and I remained cool, and while we enjoyed hanging out together on the road, everything was still platonic.

With the success of "Up, Up and Away," Soul City Records sent us out on the road to promote the record and make appearances. Limousines began picking us up at the airport to transport us to interviews at radio stations and appearances at record stores. This was something new for us.

Since Marilyn, Florence, and I had the smallest frames, we sat three abreast in the backseat while Lamonte and Ronald deposited themselves in jump seats in front of us. Those Cadillac limousines weren't much to write home about in those days—they were very uncomfortable! The long, sleek black vehicles just looked important. One time in Chicago, an interesting thing happened. The limo driver took a right turn a little too quickly, and suddenly Marilyn leaned a little more than the turn required. She snickered and excused herself, and I laughed as well. Then it happened again—another "lean" after another sharp turn, and I felt like I was definitely getting the vibe. I smiled because I wanted to see where this thing would go.

Marilyn: I was interested as well. We continued to share late-night snacks and drink Cold Duck in our hotel rooms while we were on the road. A couple of months later, we were staying in New York City. This would have probably been in July 1967. We checked into the Americana Hotel, where Billy and Ronald were sharing a room, and Florence and I roomed together. Lamonte was staying with his brother, Duck, who was now our road manager.

Anyway, one evening I decided to go down two floors and watch TV with Billy and Ronald. I immediately noticed that there wasn't much room for me, since their cramped room was furnished with just a pair of twin beds. I looked to Billy, who was lying against the headboard of his twin bed. "Mind if I join you?" I asked.

"Sure, baby," he said, as he scooted over to give me room to watch TV with him. He fluffed up a pillow and set it against the headboard for me. I kicked off my heels and hopped on the bed to watch *Gilligan's Island* or some other sitcom with them. The next thing I knew, I felt like I had fallen into a den of an octopus. First, his left arm goes around my shoulders. That was okay, but then he slid his left arm down my torso and around my waist, and that was *not* okay. This was moving a little faster than I wanted.

Billy: Give me a break. I had been drinking!

Marilyn: *What kind of woman does he think I am?* I thought. *Trying to cop a feel—and in front of Ronald!* So I got up and left in a huff. On my way back to my room, I decided this romance thing was a bad idea. The man was coarser than sandpaper and totally out of line. He must have thought I was a floozy to be carrying on like that—and we hadn't even had a date!

If that's the way he treats his women, I said to myself, *that kind of behavior won't work with me.* I decided to back off and go back to being buddies, which would probably work better for both of us and the group.

The next day, the temperature had cooled considerably in the limo drives around town. Our performance that evening went fine—the show had to go on, after all—but afterward, Billy asked whether he could come to my room and talk. I knew Florence would be there, so I figured I was safe. I said okay.

When he arrived, Billy was on his best behavior. No mention of the incident the night before; it was as if nothing happened. We sat up and talked into the wee hours. I could feel my heart melting. Florence had fallen asleep as we talked and talked—until the sunrise peaked through the window. Finally, at 6:00 a.m., we both agreed that we had better get some sleep. Billy left, never having made a move on me.

Something special was happening between us. Two weeks later, we found ourselves back in Los Angeles working at Disneyland. We sang these little three-song sets on the Tomorrowland stage (the one that rises out of the ground) every couple of hours. We thought the exposure would be good.

One night after singing at Disneyland, we were invited to a big party in Bel Air being thrown by singer Peggy Lee. She had been a sultry-throated pillar of pop music since the 1940s, so this was definitely a big invite for us—and tangible evidence that the group had arrived.

We knew this would be an A-list party, but one of our agents asked me whether he could drive me from Disneyland to Bel Air and escort me to the party. I could tell that this fellow was showing some interest in me, but I wasn't interested in him. I decided I would get Billy to drive me from Disneyland, so backstage I asked him for a ride. Billy said sure, but he added that his buddy Sonny was coming along as well, and Florence had asked him for a lift too. "That's fine with me," I said.

We drove to Peggy Lee's, and I felt like we were hanging out with the Hollywood big names now. What a special evening! I was really digging Billy's company, and we were arm in arm the entire evening. When we left the party after midnight, we took the backseat of Sonny's Pontiac. Florence sat next to him in the front seat. We dropped her off first.

Billy: While Sonny drove on, I leaned over and looked Marilyn in the eyes. Then I kissed her, and shortly after that, Sonny swerved. It seems that he had been looking in his rearview mirror, and when he saw us locking lips, he nearly wrecked the car. My roommate couldn't believe what he was seeing. After we dropped Marilyn off, he said, "Hey, man. What's going on here?"

"Well, something's happening." I laughed like a schoolkid, but at the same time, I was a little wary. *You've just kissed one of your best friends. What is she thinking right now?*

I really wondered if things were going to be all right. When I saw Marilyn the next day, everything was okay. It was a strange thing to go from good buddies to a love relationship, but I was glad to see it happen because I was falling for Marilyn. I swore Sonny to secrecy because I didn't want the rest of the group to find out. We knew they would be worried about how the group dynamics would change, so we kept our relationship on the QT.

Marilyn: We never asked the group how they felt when they finally found out, but I'm sure they suspected something was up. We decided to have one of those "casual" relationships that seemed to mark the Sixties. If the group thought Billy still had his girlfriends and I still had my wannabe boyfriends, that was fine with us. We would keep things cool for as long as we could because we didn't want our budding love affair to become an issue with the group.

Billy: I led a few of Marilyn's pursuers astray. Whenever one pumped me for information, I would say, "Yeah, that Marilyn sure is beautiful. She's a nice girl, but I don't think she's your type."

Marilyn: I'll tell you the extremes we went through to keep our little secret under wraps. We traveled to Springfield, Massachusetts, where Martha Raye—one of those venerable entertainers whose roots dated back to the old vaudeville days—topped the bill. We were asked to open the show, which was a wonderful opportunity for the group. Martha was a well-established and well-known actress, singer, and comedienne who could hoof a few dance steps as well. She started her career at the age of three in vaudeville shows and had recently gone to Vietnam with Bob Hope to entertain the troops, so she was very much in the public eye.

On opening night, the owners of the venue staged a big party for Martha after the show—to celebrate the start of the engagement. That night, I felt like Florence and Billy were especially friendly, a little too friendly for me. I looked over and was hurt to see Florence sitting in Billy's lap, and he wasn't discouraging her behavior. No matter how innocent it might have been, I was in love—and jealous.

Who's promoting this? I wondered. I certainly felt insecure because I wasn't sure of Billy's feelings for me. Perhaps that's because I was drinking, and I know Billy was drinking. Late that night, we returned to our hotel, and as we were walking toward the stairwell in the lobby, I turned to Billy and said, "You make up your mind right now! Who are you going to be with?"

Billy: Marilyn didn't care who heard her. Her voice rang out all over the lobby. Florence, Lamonte, Ron—everyone connected with the group heard Marilyn. I thought, *There it goes. Now everyone knows.*

"With you, baby," I heard myself saying. "With you."

Marilyn: And that's when it all came out. So much for being cool. We were out on the road during the "Summer of Love," which was what everyone was calling the summer of 1967 because of the hippie scene coming out of San Francisco. We worked good jobs here and there. We flew to Vancouver, British Colombia, where we were booked to sing at a Chinese restaurant called Mr. Kontons for a fortnight. You could say that our relationship became more serious in Canada, and the days of being "California casual" were closing.

On the way home, Billy said, "Our relationship has changed here, so I don't want all those guys coming over to your house." I guess I had been acting like someone keeping her options open. When Billy said that, I expected the other shoe to drop. Instead, that's all he had to say—he didn't want all these guys coming over to my house.

"What about you and your girlfriends?" I asked.

"Well, I'm going to straighten that up too," he said. "Just you wait and see." This was our declaration of a commitment to each other.

Billy: Poor Sonny. He liked having tons of girls dropping by the house, but when I told him I couldn't be part of that anymore, he said, "What's going to happen to all our girlfriends?"

"Hey, man, they all belong to you now," I said.

Marilyn: So now our relationship took a new direction. You know the old saying "Familiarity breeds contempt"? We started becoming *very* familiar with each other, and as we started becoming closer, we started arguing. I guess the honeymoon in our relationship was short-lived. I wouldn't say that it became a contact sport, but we began sparring with each other.

We argued about *everything*. Clothes, restaurants, friends, or whether the Dodgers would win the pennant—we tried to impose our views on each other. We argued about the clothes that Billy wore. Billy felt that I did everything wrong. If there is an easy way to get things done, he said, I'd find the hard way to get it done. Billy would stand back and say: "Can't you see—?" And then I would just explode. The one thing we didn't argue about was his love for and responsibility to his son. Steven was always important to him. I really respected him for that.

Billy: We saw things differently, that's all. I saw things my way, which happened to be the right way, so I thought it was my duty to show her where she had gone wrong. Marilyn was always finding the hardest way to do things. Watching her go through life this way frustrated me, but I thought I could handle it. The 5th Dimension was catching on, we were receiving tons of publicity and press coverage, and we were getting our act together.

Just about everything was exciting back then.

". . .I overheard this

commotion rise up

from Billy's table,

so I walked over

to investigate."

CHAPTER 6

STONED SOUL PICNIC

There'll be trains of laughter,
there'll be trains of music . . .

Marilyn: It's hard to explain the last half of the Sixties decade to someone who didn't grow up during those turbulent, exciting times. When I attempt to get my mind around that era, all I can see is a hazy psychedelic blur. This was a time when our generation was given permission to "do your own thing," and we ran with it. When Billy and I thumb through our boxes of memorabilia and look at magazine articles and pictures from the late Sixties, though, it's hard to suppress a chuckle. Not only did we look so young (well, we were young in those days), but those clothes we wore!

I credit Lamonte for our snazzy on-stage outfits. It all began when "Up, Up and Away" took flight. Lamonte, who was visually oriented and had that photographer's eye, said our mix-and-match clothes had to go now that the group was gaining traction and national recognition.

One afternoon, he led us on a field trip to several of the hippest clothing stores around—including De Voss on Sunset Boulevard. We took home everything we could lay our hands on—and afford: Pocahontas headbands, fringed leather vests, hip huggers, flared bell-bottom pants, jeans with fringe trim, shirts in bold geometric patterns, tight miniskirts that barely covered our bottoms, and Courreges white leather go-go boots that went halfway up the leg. I put my foot down, however, to purchasing unisex Nehru jackets with matching medallion necklaces. I always watched how Florence put her pieces together. She had a real flair for dressing sharp.

We had all decided it was important for us to dress in the "mod" styles popular at the time, and Florence and Lamonte said coordinated outfits would help us look more polished and professional. We discussed everything before a decision was made because the group was run democratically: The 5th Dimension didn't have a "leader." When something important came up, everyone's input was welcome, and then we voted on it. We joked that we met more often than the United Nations.

Another Lamonte gem happened when he suggested that everyone dress in black-and-white outfits—but not identical. Since this sounded like another good idea, we rummaged through our closets and put together a black-and-white ensemble for our next performance.

René DeKnight, the group's arranger and musical director, had invited a clothing designer named Boyd Clopton to one of our shows. When Boyd saw what we were trying to do with the black-and-white outfits, he caught our vision of taking a clothing theme and doing something individual with it. Boyd met with us and explained how we needed to think intentionally about the image we were trying to portray. One way or another, he preached, the public would have a perception about the 5th Dimension, and we could influence that perception through a certain look or image. That image would be transmitted through the photographic pictures we released and the clothes we wore in concert.

What Boyd said made sense to us, so we hired him to become our clothing designer. He was responsible for the famous "Indian" outfits that we wore in concert and which appeared on the cover of the 5th Dimension *Live!* album. By today's standards, our outfits weren't that outlandish, but a bit striking for sure. Our goal was to present the 5th Dimension as a class act but in a hip sort of way. The songs we chose to record built upon this strategy: We would present an upbeat, positive tempo that appealed to all colors.

It was great having Lamonte around whenever we did publicity work. He played the role of art director with the photographers by positioning the members of the group just so. For instance, he would place Florence and me in the foreground, front and center. Lamonte would situate his tall and lanky self on the left, set the more rotund Ronald on the right (in a way that was enhanced by Florence or me), and then position cute Billy in the center, where he mugged for the camera. Lamonte said that these shots maximized the effects of our striking costumes and our appealing physical attributes. Even back then, image was everything.

Billy: Have we talked enough about clothes? Listen, "Up, Up and Away" lifted us to another stratosphere in the pop world, and it seemed to happen so fast. Marc capitalized on our overnight success by booking us into Caesars Palace in Las Vegas—a long way from Bimbo's in San Francisco. Back in 1967, Caesars Palace was a trendsetter: the first of the big theme hotels on the Strip. Marble statues of Medici Venus, Canova Venus, Venus de Milo, David, Heve, and Bacchus were imported from Italy and situated in the foyer. Everything had a Roman décor—from the sword-and-sandal-clad centurions patrolling the gaming pits to the cocktail waitresses dressed in white togas and wearing gold wreaths in their hair. Even the parchment-like desk stationery and matchbooks came with simulated burnt edges.

We were booked to perform in Nero's Nook, which was a real happening lounge in Vegas. As soon as we arrived, the Caesars people told us,

"We had the Checkmates with Sonny Charles and Sweet Louie in here last week, and the Checkmates were really hot, so we just thought you'd want to know that since you guys are coming in behind them."

We said to ourselves that the only thing we could do was go in there and give it a try, and we wrecked the place. We worked three shows a night, six nights a week. Our first performance started at 12:30 at night, and then we took a break until our second show at 3:30 a.m., and then we finished up with a 4:40 show in the early morning, which ended at daybreak. We were never in bed before 8:00 a.m.

Marilyn: This was our first time performing in Las Vegas, where I learned something new about Billy: He liked to gamble. First, some background. By this time, we had set things up financially to pay ourselves a weekly salary of $400. Remember, this was 1967, and credit cards were just catching on, so it was fairly normal to walk around with several hundred dollars in your pocket to pay for things.

To keep our money safe while we were onstage, Billy would stuff my money inside his left boot and stick his walking-around cash in his right boot. That wasn't a bad idea, especially since we were using hotel rooms as our dressing rooms. It was never a good idea to leave cash in your hotel room since there were so many pass keys circulating.

One night, during the long break between the 12:30 a.m. and 3:30 a.m. shows, Billy tested his latest strategy at the crap tables. He thought that "playing the field"—whatever that meant—would pay off big time for him. I left him alone because I didn't want to watch him lose his money. Besides, I've never been much of a gambler because I hated losing my money. I'd rather spend it on something tangible—like clothes.

On this occasion, I overheard this commotion rise up from Billy's table, so I walked over to investigate.

"How ya doing, baby?" I said.

"Shhhhh. I got four hundred on the table."

"You got *what?*" I said rather loudly, causing complete silence and about ten heads to turn my way.

"Shhhhh. I got a roll coming up. I'm trying to win back my money."

Wait a minute. Something doesn't sound right, I thought. "You wouldn't be using my money to try winning back your money, would you?"

Now everyone's eyes were on us.

Billy looked at me with a mischievous grin and shook the pair of dice in his hands. Then he blew in his cupped hands and let the white cubes fly. "Come on, dice. Don't fail me now!"

The dice ricocheted off the foam wall and landed on the green felt—in the right combination. That was fortunate for him, or else he wouldn't be alive today to tell his side of the story. With one roll of the dice, he won back his $400 stake.

The croupier counted off a stack of chips, which I intercepted. "You give me back my money," I told him in a tone that said I meant business. "If you want to lose all your money, that's fine, but don't get me involved."

Billy: Everything turned out okay, didn't it? I loved the action of Las Vegas, and the gambling crowd loved the 5th Dimension. We were starting to make some noise on the Strip, and people were saying that we stole the thunder from The Checkmates. Some of the original Rat Pack members dropped by to see us—Sammy Davis Jr., Joey Bishop, Peter Lawford, and Frank Sinatra. We saw Vegas celebrities like Phyllis Diller, Alan King, and Buddy Greco in the audience. We had all these famous people dropping by after they performed in the main showrooms, and that goes to your head.

After we did so well in Nero's Nook, Caesars Palace decided to bring us back into the big showroom (called the Circus Maximus), which was just unheard of after playing one time in the Nook. Then somebody came up with the bright idea of having us headline the first show and then performing as the opening act for the biggest headliner of the day—Frank Sinatra—in the second show.

Marilyn: Open for Frank Sinatra? Are you kidding me? We got our big chance on a bill that included Jose Feliciano, comedian Pat Henry, and the Harry James Orchestra. We performed after Pat Henry, and when we were done, we sat out in the house wherever we could find a seat to watch Sinatra sing. My goodness, he had an aura about him. With Frank Sinatra, you felt like you were in the company of hipness. Frank Sinatra would get up there and tell his stories, and the way he'd conduct the orchestra by snapping his fingers was really cool. I know music was changing back then, but Frank Sinatra was still perceived as very hip even in his early fifties, which was his age then.

Billy: Well, maybe females felt that way, but to males, he was just another guy, because—

Marilyn: But a lot of men liked him.

Billy: Sure they liked him, but not for the same reasons. I liked him because I enjoyed his singing, and I enjoyed how he told a story. But as for him being hip . . . well, he was hip in his way and for his time; I'll give him that.

Marilyn: This is one of the ongoing conflicts Billy and I have. We perceived hipness differently. Billy was St. Louis hip—enough said. Anyway, we got to talk with Frank and spend some time with him, but I was a little crushed when Frank became interested in Florence instead of me. Not that I ever desired any kind of relationship with him, but from an ego standpoint . . .

Billy: Wait a minute. How did he show interest in Florence?

Marilyn: He spent time talking to her. He made it very clear that he was interested in Florence. Neither of them were married at the time. Sometimes if we were standing backstage, he would just go over and concentrate his energy on her. I would think, *Is he going to come over and talk to me?* And then he wouldn't. It was like, oh, okay, but I was crushed. My teenage childhood crush evaporated like an August thunderstorm on the Strip. Of course, Billy and I were going together at the time, so nothing was ever going to happen, but I was still disappointed.

One of the photos that we have up on our wall at home was taken at Caesars Palace. It shows Frank presenting the group with our first gold record for "Stoned Soul Picnic." (In case you're wondering about "Up, Up and Away," that song was certified gold at a later date because of the battling versions with the Johnny Mann Singers.) Afterward, Frank told the press, "Without a doubt, they are the freshest, most musical, and most capable group in today's bag." That was really sweet of him because he didn't have to do that, but he wanted to because he was always calling us "the kids." He came up with that pet name because we were much younger and had this childlike enthusiasm for all the wonderful things happening to us. We were constantly laughing and cutting up.

We worked with Sinatra for a month that first time around, and we met many interesting people who came backstage and became aware of the group because we were performing with Frank Sinatra. That was a big break for the 5th Dimension.

Billy: We were getting breaks all over the place. We were in demand on the college circuit—we played on so many college campuses that I thought I had gone back to school. We appeared on the *Ed Sullivan Show* a half-dozen times and made various other television appearances: *The Tonight Show* with Johnny Carson, *The Merv Griffin Show, The John Davidson Show, The Flip Wilson Show, American Bandstand, The Dinah Shore Show*, and television specials hosted by Frank Sinatra, Woody Allen, and Burt Bacharach. We even hosted our own TV specials, "The 5th Dimension: An Odyssey in the Cosmic Universe of Peter Max," and "The 5th Dimension's Traveling Sunshine Show." We also did one-nighters around the country, stayed in Vegas for month-long engagements at Caesars, and hit the occasional state fair. Well, touring and performing is what I always wanted to do, and I was having a good time.

In the midst of all this, the sunny optimism of "Up, Up and Away" clouded over when Martin Luther King Jr. was shot at a Memphis motel on April 4, 1968. Like all black Americans, I was really upset to learn of the news. Several months later, when Democratic presidential candidate Robert Kennedy was shot and killed at the Ambassador Hotel not far from our home in Los Angeles, I knew the country was in real trouble.

We got our own personal eyeful of the political unrest sweeping the country during the Democratic Party's 1968 convention in Chicago. In those days, the convention activities were held during the day, and then in the evening, there would be various entertainment events for the delegates and party officials. We were invited to perform at the Auditorium Theater in downtown Chicago by someone high up in the Democratic Party. We showed up for the job, and we were backstage getting ready and doing meet-and-greets with various people. I remember a bunch of Democratic US senators and congressmen coming backstage to say hello.

We were doing the grip-and-grin thing when someone ran into our dressing room and told us we had to evacuate the building RIGHT AWAY!

When I asked why, I was told that someone had detonated a stink bomb in the auditorium and the whole place was in turmoil. We ran out the back door, where a limousine was waiting for us, and the driver drove us into the middle of the Chicago riots. We witnessed the Yippies clashing with police, who wielded their nightsticks with crushing authority. Meanwhile, we were scared to death. We huddled up in the limousine and wondered if we would get out of there alive.

The driver managed to maneuver us through the confusion and deposit us back at our hotel, where we watched the Chicago riot on television. All we knew was we were thankful we were no longer in the middle of that mess.

Marilyn: We had our own worries, which mainly centered around our second album. Since we had struck lightning in a bottle with songwriter Jimmy Webb—he wrote half the songs on our debut album, including "Up, Up and Away"—everyone agreed that if it ain't broke, don't fix it.

But then Jimmy and Johnny Rivers had a falling out over publishing rights, which threatened our new album. The group was excited to work with Jimmy again, and he wanted badly to work with us, so he and Johnny came to an agreement just for this album, after which Jimmy left to work with other artists.

This was our first project with Bones Howe as the producer, who knew how to keep a budget under control. One of Johnny Rivers' concerns with Jimmy was the cost it would require to produce the lush arrangements that he heard in his head, so there were monetary matters to consider. So we rolled up our sleeves and went to work on *The Magic Garden*, with Jimmy writing *eleven* of the twelve songs. The only non–Jimmy Webb song was a cover of "Ticket to Ride" by the Beatles.

Jimmy approached this as a theme album, and he composed short musical interludes that carried the listener from song to song, story to story, vignette to vignette. These striking interludes between songs effectively simulated one long suite of music about Jimmy's unrequited love between himself and a young woman named Susan.

Billy and I consider *The Magic Garden* to be the group's finest work, which is why it mystifies us that the album didn't do as well as we had hoped. We expected it to have a major impact on the market, but it didn't happen. In a sense, *The Magic Garden* ended up being an underground success, and to this day we love listening to that album.

Billy: We charted only two songs off *The Magic Garden*—"Paper Cup" and "Carpet Man"—but this pair *barely* cracked the Top 40. Maybe we had hit the famous "sophomore slump" that we had heard about in the industry.

Since Jimmy departed to work with different artists, we began looking around for new songwriters for us to partner with. As word got around in the industry, a manager named David Geffen approached Bones Howe about the 5th Dimension working with a young songwriter named Laura Nyro.

I recognized that name! Back when we had played Bimbo's in San Francisco, I had bumped into her at the Hyde Park Apartments, where the guys and I were staying. Her room was right above ours, and I could hear her singing and working on some songwriting project. She looked the part of a hippie troubadour—flowing, funky skirts and long, loose hair parted

in the middle. She had written her first hit, "And When I Die"—popu-
larized by Peter, Paul, and Mary and Blood, Sweat, and Tears—when she
was a tender seventeen-year-old from New York City.

She wasn't much older—only twenty years old—when Laura began
working with us on our third album. She wrote two great songs that turned
out to be hits—a catchy tune called "Stoned Soul Picnic" and "Sweet
Blindness." The bigger hit was "Stoned Soul Picnic," which may sound like
a bunch of people getting drunk at a lazy picnic, but that wasn't the case.
Actually, this song—like many that she wrote—blended folk, jazz, soul,
gospel, and Broadway swing with quirky, soulful lyrics:

Can you surrey,
Can you picnic?
Can you surrey,
Can you picnic?

Surrey down to a stoned soul picnic
Surrey down to a stoned soul picnic
There'll be lots of time and wine
Red yellow honey
Sassafras and moonshine
Red yellow honey
Sassafrass and moonshine
Stoned soul
Surrey down to a stoned soul picnic
Surrey down to a stoned soul picnic

The engaging melody and infectious groove carried the song, and we
made it the title cut of our third album. The song released several weeks
after Robert Kennedy's assassination, which makes me think that maybe

"Stoned Soul Picnic" was the type of upbeat song that gave people a lift during a dark period in our nation's history. When "Stoned Soul Picnic" shot up to No. 3 on the Billboard Top 40, we were back in business. We would never be called "one-hit wonders" now.

Marilyn: So our career was back on track, and more importantly, so was our love affair. Billy and I had been together for nearly a year, and our relationship had never interfered professionally with the group. Besides, there was another budding love match brewing: Our manager, Marc, and our very own Florence had fallen in love as well. Since Ronald was already spoken for with Bobette, that left Lamonte unattached, but that was fine with him. He preferred being footloose and fancy free.

We were having the time of our lives, and if there's a story that captures the party mood of the late Sixties, this is it. One time, we were asked to open for the Temptations in San Francisco. We boarded a short PSA flight from LAX to SFO, but someone was missing—Billy. We flew ahead and got word that he would grab a later flight and meet us at the Fillmore Auditorium.

Billy grabbed a taxi at the San Francisco airport and asked to be dropped off at the Fillmore. When the taxi entered the Haight-Ashbury district, the mecca of flower power and the central gathering point for hippies, there was such an air of excitement in the streets that Billy said to the cabbie, "That's close enough; you can let me off here. I'll find the Fillmore on foot."

"Suit yourself," said the cab driver as he collected his fare and tip.

Walking through Haight-Ashbury was a revelation to Billy. Everywhere he looked, young people were hanging out of the windows of their walk-up apartments or congregating on the stairs while loud rock music blasted the neighborhood.

Billy: Everyone was doing their thing. They were passing around joints, and when I walked by, they asked me to join them. "Take a hit, brother," they said, so I did my thing. A few tokes here and a few tokes there, and I was feeling good, and they were feeling good. Everyone I ran into was so loving—quite a contrast to all the racial ugliness the country had been through. I ended up hanging out for several hours with my new-found friends, taking hits of their marijuana and drinking cheap wine.

I don't know how I remembered to look at my watch in my stoned condition, but when I did, there were enough brain cells working to remind me that I needed to get to the concert on time. I managed to find the Fillmore Auditorium, which made this my lucky day. When I arrived stoned and giggling, I told Marilyn and the others what a great time I had in Haight-Ashbury. They sure gave me a lot of funny looks that night.

Marilyn: Although Billy and I smoked pot in our time, we were not classic "potheads," and in fact, that really wasn't our scene. (For the record, the other members of the 5th Dimension did not indulge.) I remember us doing a concert with Sonny and Cher and some other acts at Mount Tamalpais, located near the southern tip of the Marin Peninsula, the northernmost of the two peninsulas that nearly enclose San Francisco Bay.

As you would expect, we drew a young, pot-smoking, hippie crowd, and many of the acts were getting high backstage before their performances. We chose not to do that, although Billy had been drinking during the day. But I knew that being in an altered state of consciousness before a performance didn't work for me. I had learned my lesson when we happened to be at Whisky A-Go-Go one time. On this occasion, a lot of friends came out to see us as this was our first major appearance in LA since we had become hot. Chums from Dorsey High dropped by, as well as some of the guys' buddies from St. Louis who had moved out West.

It turned into a big party backstage before the performance. The alcohol was flowing in some serious celebrating. Billy liked his Seagrams VO Canadian whisky. My drink of choice was screwdrivers—vodka and orange juice.

I had a good little buzz going when I took the stage. Billy began singing a song, and I was singing background with the others when I remember thinking, *I cannot hear myself*. I didn't know whether I was too loud, if I was blending with the others, if my timing was right, or if I was in tune.

I began to realize that by drinking and partying before we went on stage, I was not doing my best, but performing was what I always wanted to do! Singing in public had been my life's desire since I was a little girl. I said to myself, *I'm not going to blow this opportunity to become a success by drinking and having a good time before I go on stage. I can drink and have a good time when I come off*. That was a powerful moment for me, to make a decision of how I would approach my work in the music business.

Billy: I understood Marilyn's feelings because I had a similar experience with weed. The common belief was that you were more creative in this heightened state of mind. Guys would say, "Hey, you can play better when you smoke weed. You can dance better. You can sing better." I didn't find that to be true.

Smoking weed made me lazy. I knew there were certain steps that everybody was supposed to make, but when I smoked pot before a show, my mind said, *You don't have to make that step*. I felt like I was cheating the rest of the group when I smoked pot before a show. If I couldn't perform in a professional manner on stage, I didn't belong up there.

Marilyn: It's good that Billy and I and the rest of the group had our heads screwed on pretty straight because we were about to enter the white-hot zone that only a No. 1 hit record can bring.

If there was ever a song that summed up where this country was at in 1969, it was the song "Aquarius/Let the Sun Shine In."

"Don't ask me where that

last lyric came from—

it was totally unplanned,

but for more than thirty years,

people have told me that's the

lyric that resonated with them."

CHAPTER 7

THOSE
WERE THE
DAYS

*For we were young and sure
to have our way . . .*

Billy: In the fall of 1968, we returned to New York City for a series of performances at the Royal Box, a venue at the Americana Hotel on 7th Avenue and 52nd Street in midtown Manhattan. Normally, a group doesn't return to the same city so soon after having performed there earlier in the year, but we had to cancel several shows in June after Florence and I encountered vocal problems. Working on the recording of the *Stoned Soul Picnic* album in the afternoon and singing two performances at the Royal Box at night proved to be too much of a strain on our voices.

I had some errands to run on this October afternoon, so I hailed a taxi. Upon my return to the Americana a few hours later, I reached for my wallet and noticed it wasn't in my suit coat pocket any longer.

I had no idea where I had lost my wallet—or if some light-fingered pickpocket had pinched it. "What am I going to do?" I asked Marilyn back in our hotel room. My wallet contained several hundred dollars in cash, my California driver's license, a few business cards, and my AFTRA card—my American Federation of Television and Radio Artists union card. I didn't carry any credit cards because they weren't a big deal in the late Sixties, and the phrase "identity theft" hadn't been invented yet.

"Well, you can kiss that wallet good-bye," Marilyn said. That wasn't very encouraging. Then again, we were in New York City.

Suddenly, the phone rang in our hotel room.

"Is this the big star Billy Davis, Jr.?" I heard a voice say.

"Well, yeah," I replied evenly, not sure where this was leading.

"I've got your wallet, but I'm not going to bring it over to you. You're going to have to come and get it."

This was getting interesting. "No problem," I said. "I don't care where I have to go. I'm just glad you found it. Who am I speaking to?"

"Ed Gifford."

"Ed, I'm pleased to meet you over the phone. So where should I go?"

Ed dictated his address—a midtown apartment. I took a cab over to his flat, where I met him and his wife. He explained that after he noticed my AFTRA card, he called the New York office and asked who I was. They informed him that I sang with the 5th Dimension and that we were playing at the Royal Box. Then Ed called the Americana Hotel and learned that I was staying there, so he worked pretty hard to find me. When he handed over my wallet—which he found in the back of a cab—I heard him say, "You're a lucky man."

"You got that right," I agreed. "Listen, to show my appreciation, I'd like to invite you and your wife to see the 5th Dimension."

"Hey, that sounds great," Ed said.

The following night, Ed and his wife came backstage after the show and raved about the performance. "You guys were great," he said, slapping my back. "Now you have to come see my show."

"Your show?"

"Yeah, my show. I'm one of the producers of *Hair*, the musical playing on Broadway."

Marilyn: Everyone had heard of *Hair*, which was all over the newspapers in those days. The musical was actually three shows in one: a celebration of free love and the hippie lifestyle; a satirical attack on the Establishment; and the story of one hippie's decision whether to avoid the draft and flee to Canada. *Hair* sang the praises of everything from marijuana to masturbation and pretty much thumbed its nose at traditional values.

Oh, I have to mention another little thing about *Hair*, which was billed as an "American tribal love/rock musical." At the end of act 1 under dramatic lighting, a dozen members of the cast—male and female—stood totally naked in front of the audience. This was the infamous nude scene that shocked folks in America—people naked on stage! In the "let's try anything" atmosphere of the late Sixties, however, the nudity and the musical's rebellious themes fit with the times.

The characters in the play certainly delivered some clever lines. In discussing Vietnam, one of the characters said, "The draft is white people sending black people to fight yellow people to protect the country they stole from the red people." The protest themes—as well as the promise to witness actors in full frontal nudity—propelled the rock musical into a huge success off and on Broadway.

Naturally, I was curious to see *Hair*, as was Billy. We were excited to hear that Ed was inviting the entire 5th Dimension to a nearly sold-out matinee. Although we couldn't sit together, I was enthralled when Ronnie Dyson sang the lead in the opening song called "Age of Aquarius." The guy had a beautiful voice, and I was quite impressed.

Billy: That Ronnie had some pipes, all right. During the intermission, we caught up with Lamonte, Ronald, and Florence in the lobby, and we all raved about what we had seen, especially the opening number, "Age of Aquarius."

"We've got to record that song," I said to the others. "There's no doubt in my mind that 'Aquarius' is a hit."

The group was in complete agreement. "Aquarius" was such a great song that we had to record it as soon as possible.

The next day, I called Los Angeles and spoke with our producer, Bones Howe. I was so excited I could barely talk. "Bones, you won't believe what we did yesterday. We went to see *Hair*, and there's this song that's going to be a dynamite hit for us. It's called the 'Age of Aquarius.'"

There was a pause on the phone. "Well, I don't know," Bones replied. "That song's been recorded three times, and nobody's been able to get a hit on it."

"I don't care if no one's gotten a hit off that song," I shot back. "We can make it one. I just know it!"

I could hear Bones thinking, which was a good sign. "Tell you what. Let me think about it. Maybe there's something we can do to freshen it up a bit."

Marilyn: A couple of weeks later, Bones called us back and said, "I think I've come up with an idea about how we can make this song work."

"Really? What would that be, Bones?" I had witnessed dozens of times when Bones came up with just the right arrangement or just the right sound for our recordings.

"I'm toying with adding 'Let the Sun Shine In' to the last part of the song—really finish on a high note."

That was an intriguing idea. Those two songs were *Hair*'s bookends, so to speak, since the musical opened with "Age of Aquarius" and finished with "Let the Sun Shine In," but I didn't care what song he paired it with—I just wanted to record "Aquarius."

Billy: I immediately understood why Bones wanted to add "Let the Sun Shine In." He wanted to create some excitement toward the end of the song, give it a real lift. We were all interested in how this marriage between "Age of Aquarius" and "Let the Sun Shine In" would work when we could finally schedule some time in the studio.

Marilyn: A month later, we were in Las Vegas opening for Frank Sinatra at Caesars Palace. Bones flew over from Los Angeles with the tracks to "Aquarius," which he had recorded with some of LA's top session players—Hal Blaine, Joe Osbourne, and Larry Knechtel. Bones rented a funky recording studio not far from the Strip that happened to back up to several train tracks. Also in the studio that day was Bob Alcivar, who did most of our vocal arrangements whenever we recorded. He had Florence and me sing the opening verse together:

When the moon is in the seventh house
And Jupiter aligns with Mars
Then peace will guide the planets
And love will fill the stars

Florence and I took several takes, and I know this sounds hard to believe, but we had to stop singing our biggest hit every time the trains passed by. Bob thought our voices blended beautifully, and when we listened to the playback, it sounded like a 5th Dimension approach.

Billy: We continued to lay down background vocals throughout the rest of "Age of Aquarius" and "Let the Sun Shine In." Bones used an additional track to "double" our voices—to make the chorus lines sound like ten people were singing, not five. When we were done, Bones gathered us into the control booth and played the "Let the Sun Shine In" section. Then he turned to me and said, "Billy, I want you to go out there and sing some adlibs over this. Anything that comes to your mind, you just go for it." Coming from a gospel background, adlibs were easy for me to hear in my head, and I was usually asked to sing them whenever we wanted to create excitement and give our pop songs a more soulful feel.

I took my spot in the studio and put on a set of headphones to listen to the playback. I could see Marilyn and the rest of the group through the window into the control room, and I could tell by their body language that they were getting excited while I really went for it with everything I had:

Everyone just sing along
And let the sun shine in
Open up your heart
And let the sun shine in

A great moment for all of us, receiving our star on the Hollywood Walk of Fame, in 1991. *(HCOC publicity photo)*

Reunion of the original 5th Dimension, 1991. *(James Loy)*

ABOVE: Having a special meeting with Pope John Paul II in San Antonio, where we performed for him, 1987. (*L'Osservatore Romano Citta' del Vaticano; Servizio Fotografico, Arturo Mari*)

RIGHT: The Marilyn McCoo & Billy Davis, Jr Show, on CBS-TV, summer of 1977. Billy's tuxedo was designed by Joe Cotroneo, and Marilyn's outfit was a Ray Aghayan creation. (*CBS-TV publicity photo*)

ABOVE: An intimate moment. (*Lamonte McLemore*)

RIGHT: Here I am at 8 years old in a family portrait: my brother, Wayman, at my mother's side, sister Millie not thrilled about the whole idea, me (with glasses!), Glenda, and Daddy. (*Arlin Studio, Los Angeles*)

ABOVE: With President and Mrs. George Bush at the 1989 official Christmas tree lighting ceremony, after our performance. (*Official White House photograph*)

ABOVE: The group in a scene from our second TV special: The 5th Dimension's Traveling Sunshine Show" *(Ian Samson)*

RIGHT: With Magic Johnson and vocal group Friends of Distinction founder, Harry Elston, at a Los Angeles Raiders game, after we sang the National Anthem.

With our parents at our wedding reception. (*Cliff Hall*)

Florence, Ronald, Lamont, and our musical director, Rene deKnight, were there to help us celebrate our wedding day. Florence, too, was a bride, having wed the group's manager, Marc Gordon, two weeks earlier. (*Cliff Hall*)

To Billy Davis Jr.
With Appreciation,

Laura Bush *George W. Bush*

ABOVE: With President and Mrs. George W. Bush at a pre-inaugural concert, following the performance. (*Official White House photograph*)

RIGHT: With my singing group, the Emeralds, before we switched to gospel. I'm the one on the bottom.

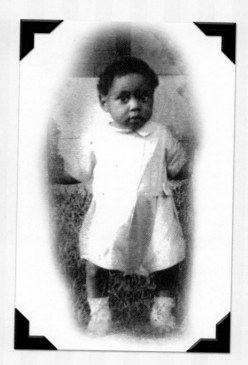

ABOVE LEFT: Marilyn, surveying the world around her, in Columbus, GA, at 6 months.

ABOVE RIGHT: Billy at age 1, learning to walk in St. Louis.

LEFT: Our son, Steven, at age 11 (*Drewry Photocolor Corp.*)

With actor Anthony Quinn at an art exhibit of his work in Hawaii. We bought one of his sculptures. (*Photowork*)

Randy Jeffries, our dedicated friend and assistant.

Winning the 1976 Grammy Award as an R&B duet for "You Don't Have to Be a Star", with singer Peter Frampton, who presented it to us. (*Peter C. Borsari*)

In a skit from our short-lived CBS televison series with terrific, new, as yet undiscovered talents: Jay Leno, Tim Reid and Lewis Arquette. *(CBS-TV publicity photo)*

Our very special friends Frank and Bunny Wilson, enjoying a meal at our house.

Lillian Hawkins who took care of our son, Steven, and us; with our dog Oro, who was a gift from friends Nina and Roger at Solid Gold.

LEFT: With Andy Gibb, performing our hosting duties on Solid Gold, 1981. (*Operation Prime Time publicity photo*)

BELOW: In 1999, two weeks prior to Billy's prostate surgery, backstage at the taping of "The Jamie Foxx Show", with Jamie Foxx and our granddaughter, Stephanie.

ABOVE: Caught in a huddle with Ben Vereen and Los Angeles Mayor Tom Bradley.

RIGHT: Here we are, the Davis family, as adults. Left to Right (seated on floor): sisters Norzora, Velura, and Fedora; (second row) Mother and Daddy; (standing in back) brothers Ronald, Wilbert, Arthur and me.

LEFT: Celebrating Billy's "49 $^{11}/_{12}$" birthday party. *(Ron Wolfson)*

BELOW: With Stevie Wonder, sharing a funny moment backstage at an awards show.

Backstage in Las Vegas at the Desert Inn Hotel with Liza Minelli and Lou Rawls.
(*Cashman Photo Enterprises*)

At the White House in 1969. President and Mrs. Nixon and daughter, Tricia, thank the group for our performance before fifty governors and their wives.
(*Official White House photo*)

LEFT: With the best man at our wedding and now our road manager, Sonny Porter, with us on tour.

BELOW: Frank Sinatra presents to the group our first gold record, "Stoned Soul Picnic", on the stage of Ceasar's Palace in Las Vegas. We are wearing a Boyd Clopton creation. Left to right: Ronald, Florence, Billy, Sinatra, Marilyn, Lamonte. (D. Cropper)

In my role as "Julie" in the revival of "Showboat" on Broadway, 1995. (*Livent Productions publicity photo*)

With Gail Deadrick, our dear friend and musical director of almost 20 years, back-stage at the Desert Inn, Las Vegas, 1989.

Guest appearance on "Christmas in Washington" TV special hosted by President and Mrs. Ronald Reagan, with Sara Boyers, who was my manager.

At the 1967 Grammy Awards where "Up, Up and Away" won six awards. The 5th Dimension celebrate with songwriter, Jimmy Webb and Liberty Records executives in Boyd Clopton outfits designed for the occasion. Left to right: Billy, Ronald, Macey Lipman (head of marketing and promotion), Marilyn, Jimmy Webb, Al Bennett (President of Liberty Records), Florence and Lamonte. *(Liberty Records publicity photo)*

With then Chairman of the Joint Chiefs of Staff General and Mrs. Colin Powell at a USO anniversary celebration honoring the general. *(USO publicity photo)*

When you are lonely
And friends turn their back to you
Open up your heart and let the sun shine in.
You've got to feeeeel it
I want you to sing along with the 5th Dimension—AAAHHHH!

Don't ask me where that last lyric came from—it was totally unplanned, but for more than thirty years, people have told me that's the lyric that resonated with them—*I want you to sing along with the 5th Dimension* . . . because it was totally off the wall.

I also don't know where that primal scream came from, but I'm telling you, that's the most fun I ever had adlibbing a song. I did it in three or four takes, and Bones engineered everything just right. He was a master technician, considering how primitive the technology was back then compared to today.

Marilyn: I remember sitting in the engineering room with Bones watching Billy just let go. "Bones, you gotta use that line," I said, and the others in the group agreed with me.

We all believed that "Aquarius/Let the Sun Shine In" sounded like a hit to us, but you never took anything for granted in our business. That's why it was a tremendously exciting moment to watch this song shoot to the top of the Billboard Top 40 in March 1969. "Aquarius" became the 5th Dimension's first No. 1 hit, staying on top of the charts for six weeks and on the Billboard Top 40 for four months. That was truly a blessing in disguise; it never would have happened if Billy hadn't lost his wallet.

Having a No. 1 hit created *much* more demand on our time—interviews, photo features, appearances, concerts, phone calls, agents, and a million people to greet. Paparazzi suddenly wanted to take *our* pictures.

The white-hot glare of the media was intense, but we didn't mind because we were running so fast that we didn't have time to think.

Billy and I felt like our relationship was pretty hot too. Right around the time we recorded "Aquarius," Billy and I were spending all of our free time together. When we were back in Los Angeles, he usually spent the night at my apartment, located in Baldwin Hills, a Los Angeles suburb not far from LAX, which was convenient for our lifestyles. An apartment worked fine since we were on the road so many months out of the year.

Billy: I still kept my apartment with Sonny, but most of the time I was at Marilyn's place. That created problems because I couldn't keep track of where my clothes were—her place or mine. I would be looking for my shoes, but my shoes would be at the other place, or the belt was over there, or something. I said to Marilyn, "I can't do this. I have to be either here or there. It's too confusing for me."

Marilyn: So we agreed that Billy would move in with me, and we lived together in the apartment building that my mother owned and also lived in. She was a bit straightlaced, so I imagined that this "living together" thing didn't sit well with her, but she never said anything to us. I think that's because she did not want to believe what was happening, so she ignored it.

One time, she flew back to New York City to see us perform at the Royal Box, the club inside the Americana Hotel. Mommy had been raised in Jersey City, New Jersey, so this was a combination homecoming and bring-all-the-relatives-to-the-show type of happening. One afternoon, we'd gone out for lunch and were strolling back to my hotel. I could tell that she wanted to see my room—probably to see whether Billy was sharing it with me. "I want to see what your room looks like," my mother said. "It must be nice."

"Oh, it is nice, Mommy, but you don't want to come all the way up to the twentieth floor to see a hotel room."

"I'm not doing anything, and I'd love to see your room."

"Mommy, it's just a hotel room—"

The next thing I knew, we were getting off the elevator, and I could see our room down at the end of the hall. *You better tell her something*, I thought. *You don't want her to walk in there with no warning.*

My mouth got dry. "Mommy, there's something I should tell you . . . you should know that . . . that Billy and I are staying together," I croaked.

Staying together. Such a nice euphemism for shacking up or whatever my mother was thinking at the time.

"Oh?" was all my mother said.

When I opened the door and saw Billy's clothes lying all over the place, I watched Mommy's eyes scan the room, then look over to the closet, where Billy's suits were hanging. The hiding was over, but she was cool about it. She acted as though it was no big thing, but it wasn't until years later I heard that after our visit, she cried her heart out at her sister's apartment. "This is terrible," she wailed to her sister, my Aunt Mil. "What's happened is awful."

"What's wrong, Mary?" her sister asked, suddenly concerned.

"Billy and Marilyn are . . . are . . . living together," she choked out between sobs.

"Is that all?" Aunt Mil wasn't fazed. "Oh, I thought someone had gotten hurt. Mary, that's what kids are doing today."

Mommy shrugged her shoulders. While she saw herself as a women's libber—as feminists called themselves in those days—and the feminist belief system said women should feel "liberated" enough to do what they want in a sexual relationship—living together still didn't sit well with her.

After that incident, Billy felt like he couldn't keep the news from his parents. One afternoon, he was on the phone talking to his father in St. Louis. "Hold on a second, Daddy. I want you to say hi to my roommate."

Roommate? I thought. *What was up with that?* Then my blood began to boil because I thought he was disrespecting me. "No, you talk to your father," I hissed, but I took the phone because his father was waiting. "Hello, Mr. Davis."

Billy stood by, cracking up like a sixth-grader, while I spoke nothing but sweetness to his father. As soon as I placed the phone back in its cradle, I gave him a piece of my mind. I was furious!

Initially, my mother didn't hassle me about getting married, and I think that's because she always said that she would never do that to her daughters. That line of reasoning lasted about two months, however.

One day over the phone, she broached the rather delicate subject. "Um, do you think you and Billy will ever get married?" she wondered.

"Mommy, I don't want to talk about getting married, and you told me that you were never going to ask me about getting married, so what's it going to be?"

"Well, yeah, but I did not expect you to be *living* with somebody."

"Oh, so that's it. A piece of paper would make you happy?"

I wasn't anxious to marry Billy because my mother and father had split up a few years earlier, right around the same time as my godmother and her husband split up. I did not see any reason why I should mess up a good relationship by getting married. There was no reason to rush to the altar, especially because the ink was barely dry on Billy's divorce decree from

Edna. After a four-year separation, their divorce became final in early 1969. We had seen our share of celebrity marriages split up, and we didn't want to become one of those statistics. In addition, by marrying Billy, I would become an instant wife and mother to his son, Steven. I had met Steven before, but he lived with his mother in St. Louis, and we hadn't had much time to get to know each other.

In April 1969, we flew up to Vancouver, British Colombia, to perform at a nightclub called The Cave. We weren't the happiest of campers to be back in a nightclub. We had a No. 1 hit on our hands, and now we had to fulfill an old commitment to play there—and two shows a night!

During our engagement, the group, along with our manager Marc Gordon, was invited to a private barbecue on our day off at the home of Jack and Marlene Cohen, who had an awesome house. We were having a nice time standing around with drinks in our hands and admiring the view when someone tinkled a glass with a knife.

"Everybody, if I can have your attention please," Marc said, clearing his throat. "I would like to introduce the woman who said yes to my marriage proposal—Florence LaRue!"

Marc and Florence were getting married! The news didn't come as a total surprise since Billy and I knew that where there was smoke, a fire was sure to appear. Still, the announcement caught us off guard. We congratulated the prospective bride and groom, but I don't think more than fifteen minutes passed before several acquaintances asked, "So, when are you two getting married?"

"It's wonderful that they're getting married," I replied, pointing my champagne glass toward the happy couple. "We're not ready."

When we got back to our hotel room, I could tell something was different about Billy. "You know, baby, I've been thinking about it," he said.

"You've been thinking about what?"

"Maybe we should go and do the thing."

"Do what thing?"

"You know, get married. What do you think?"

His proposal was heartfelt because I knew his hesitancy meant that he was nervous. I didn't know what to think though because his proposal scared me. As the options tumbled through my mind, I realized that if I said no, I would lose him. If I said yes, I feared we could end up getting a divorce. True, couples got divorced every day, but it wasn't what I wanted.

"Yeah—okay," I said with a happy and anxious heart.

Billy: We celebrated when Marilyn slapped a big wet kiss on my lips. She laid one on me, I can tell you that. But you know what? I wasn't thinking about divorce when I asked Marilyn to marry me. I knew we would be married forever. Splitting up with Edna had been painful enough, and I didn't want to go through that again.

Marilyn: The first person I called was my mother because I knew she would be thrilled to hear that her daughter was getting married.

"Mommy, I have something to tell you," I announced over the phone.

"What?"

"Billy and I are getting married."

Pause.

"Mommy?"

"Yes."

"I thought you'd be happy. You've been bugging me about getting married."

The silence evaporated. She paused and said, "Well, it's not every day that a daughter calls and says that she's getting married."

"Aren't you going to say something?"

"What am I supposed to say?"

"Well, congratulations would be nice."

"Okay, congratulations." *So there.*

The discussion soon turned to *where* and *when* we would be getting married. I knew what I *didn't* want to do, and that was to get married in a hot air balloon, which Marc and Florence were planning to do. Both of us were terrified of heights.

The *where* was the easy part—we'd get married in Los Angeles, which was also close to my parents. *When* would prove to be more troublesome. Remember, this was the spring of 1969, and we were riding a No. 1 hit. We looked at our itinerary and saw that in July, we would be singing a one-week engagement at the Greek Theater in Los Angeles, followed by a week off.

When we informed the group about our marriage plans, they didn't know whether to say congratulations or ask where they could send their condolences. All they saw was a couple who constantly argued. To tell you the truth, we did argue about *everything*, large and small. The group members, our friends, and our musicians teased us about our arguing.

One time I was hospitalized for two weeks while the group went on the road without me. Rudy Stevenson, our guitar player, teased Billy about missing me so much that my husband-to-be argued with the empty seat next to him on the tour bus.

Billy and I both had opinions on how this relationship should proceed, as you would expect. While we knew our love for each other was tender and real, we both thought we were right when it came to business and personal matters. Neither of us liked to give in.

Billy did have the wisdom to step aside and let my mother and me plan our wedding. We decided that The Church of Christian Fellowship in South Central LA would be a wonderful place to exchange our vows. I never felt like this was just my wedding, though. When it came to things like choosing our china and silver patterns—things we would be living with—I didn't make any final selections until Billy saw and approved them.

About a month before the wedding day, I became very frightened that I was making the wrong choice, that I was being carried along by all the excitement of two weddings taking place in the group and the accompanying hoopla in the press. What flat-out scared me was the prospect of actually getting *married*.

I dropped by my mother's apartment one time when Billy wasn't around (remember, we lived in the same complex), and I was a jumble of tears.

"What's wrong?" my mother soothed.

"I don't know if I should be doing this or not," I sniffled. "Maybe I'm making a huge mistake marrying Billy."

My mother appeared calm. "Okay, tell me why you think it's a mistake. Let's begin with you telling me all the things that you think are wrong with Billy."

So I talked about the fact that we came from different backgrounds, that I had a college education and he had only finished high school, and he liked to drink. I added that we seemed to argue continually.

"Well, it takes time to get to know each other," my mother said. "Yes, you do seem to argue a lot, but I think that will eventually pass. And I have noticed that he drinks a bit. Now tell me all the good things about Billy."

My attitude brightened. "Billy's thoughtful and kind. He's generous. I can talk to him about anything. He understands women, and I think he understands me more than any guy I've known before. We have the same outlook on life—and we share the same passion for music. He's open to trying new things, like going to a Japanese restaurant or seeing a foreign film."

"Well, Marilyn, what you've described are some of the most important qualities in a man. If you can find a man who is kind, considerate, and generous—and really loves you—then those are the most important things. You will never find a knight in shining armor. You're never going to marry someone who's perfect. After all, I'm sure there are things about you that get on his nerves."

"Impossible," I said, crossing my arms. Then I laughed. I felt like a sack of flour had been taken off my shoulders. After that conversation, I was at peace. I knew then that I had made the right choice.

On the day before our wedding, Billy and I drove to Los Angeles International Airport to pick up one of Billy's friends, Ron Waldroup, who was flying in from Las Vegas. Billy had gotten to know Ron, who tended bar at Caesars Palace, while he bent his elbow after our shows at Nero's Nook. We found Ron outside the terminal at LAX, where he hopped into our car with one piece of luggage.

We were driving north on the San Diego Freeway when Billy and I began sniping at each other. I told him that he had better not drink before the church ceremony, but he replied that he would do what he pleased, and we got into one of our typical rows. Ron, sitting in the back, swiveled his head back and forth as we raised the temperature inside that car about four hundred degrees. I didn't care if we had an audience; this was war!

Billy: Marilyn always had something to say about everything. She always had to be right, and she was continually on my case. She was always saying I was too loud, I drank too much, I embarrassed her . . . You get the idea.

Maybe it was prewedding jitters, but Marilyn and I must have had a particularly bad day when we picked up Ron at LAX. "For God's sake, you're getting married. What are you doing?" Ron demanded from the backseat of my Camaro.

"What do you mean, Ron?" I asked.

"Come on, guys, I didn't come all the way from Las Vegas to hear you two argue," he said. "If this the way you're going to act, I'm going back home."

I didn't believe Ron when he said he'd fly back home—after all, we had just picked him up at the airport—but I heard what he was saying: Our arguing made him feel uncomfortable. So Marilyn and I called a truce, which lasted all of five minutes. We picked up our old argument about my drinking in no time!

"That's it," Ron said, slamming the back of our seat. "Take me back to the airport."

"You're kidding, Ron," I said, cracking a smile. "The wedding's tomorrow."

"I don't care. Take me back to LAX. I'm serious."

"Ron, you cannot be serious—"

"With you two guys? Sure, I'm serious."

We couldn't talk Ron out of changing his mind, so we got off the next exit and reversed our direction. That Camaro became awfully quiet for the next half hour. True to his word, Ron flew back to Las Vegas and missed our wedding.

That incident symbolized the type of turmoil bubbling underneath the surface of our relationship.

Marilyn: They say the day a woman gets married is the happiest day of her life. Certainly when I look through my wedding album, warm memories flood my heart. I *loved* my wedding dress—ah, outfit. I did not wear a traditional dress, but I did want to be married in white. I wore a white lace two-piece outfit with a long tunic and see-through pants with bell-bottom flares topped off with a white chiffon headband that hung down my back, all designed by Boyd Clopton. Hey, this was the Age of Aquarius, and Billy and I had decided that we would exchange wedding bands with our astrological signs inscribed on them—he was a Cancer and I was a Libra.

One of the traditional things I *did* do that day was not see Billy in the morning. Maybe I should have kept an eye on him. After my father walked me down the aisle and handed me off to Billy with a warm kiss, I looked into Billy's . . . bloodshot eyes. His buddies had taken him out the night before, and he still showed the effects of his celebration.

I had begged him not to drink before the wedding, and he honored that. But by the time we took photos around the wedding cake, he had made up for lost time. As the photographer snapped pictures, I told him through smiling, clenched teeth how disappointed I was because he was getting smashed. "You're messing up our wedding," I said.

Billy: Yeah, I had been drinking. But hey, I had to celebrate getting married. Drinkers always find a reason to celebrate. My balance wasn't bolstered when Marilyn's godmother kept handing me glasses of champagne fortified with vodka. I drank a bunch of those, thinking, *Oh, boy, these are good.*

A honeymoon was also a great reason to celebrate, and we planned that well too. Since the 5th Dimension had been booked for several dates in Honolulu right after our wedding, I saw this as a great way to combine work and a honeymoon because we had another week off following the Honolulu dates.

Marilyn and I flew over to Maui for the day to visit some friends, the Kennedys, who lived on the island. They immediately wanted to take us to a private cove not far from their home. As the women put together a picnic basket in the kitchen, Mike Kennedy pulled me over. "What do you say we do some scuba diving? It's like swimming in a fish tank out there," he said, gesturing toward the horizon.

"I've never done scuba diving," I said.

"Don't worry about it," he said. "I have these special masks that hook up to a generator on the surface of the water. I'll show you how to do it. It's easy."

Mike walked me out to his garage, where a generator sat inside an inner tube. He gave me some basic instruction about what to do, and he made it sound so simple. He said the air would be fed into our masks by tubes connected to the generator floating atop the ocean surface.

Mike had some last-minute advice for me. "Whatever you do, don't touch your mask. I don't care if you have an itch, don't shift your mask around."

"Got it," I said.

When we got down to the beach, Mike and I put on swim fins and thirty-two-pound weight belts. I clutched a spear gun in my right hand.

We set off into the azure blue Pacific, and I immediately loved the underwater environment. Everything I saw through my mask was just beautiful, and I loved the way the sun rays streaked through the water and the way stingrays floated by. Tropical fish in orange and yellow hues swam in schools around the reefs.

We swam into deeper and deeper waters to around twenty-five feet of depth. I felt comfortable following Mike because he had done this before. The only irksome thing was this itch on the side of my nose. *You're not going to touch it*, I said to myself. Mind over matter. I hadn't forgotten that Mike said not to touch the mask.

The same itch came back, but this time the urge to scratch was over-whelming. I fought and fought the urge . . . until I thought just a little scratch might make it go away. *Boom!* Water shot into my mask, and in an instant, my world was a blur.

I knew what to do. I had to swim to the surface as quickly as I could. I started pumping my legs, but I didn't go anywhere. *How come I'm not going to the top?* After ten, fifteen seconds of furiously pumping, I was still getting nowhere, and panic rose in my throat. I was going to drown!

Mike happened to turn around, and if he hadn't, I wouldn't be alive today. He immediately assessed the situation: I couldn't rise to the top because of my iron belt. He rushed over, snapped loose my belt, and I shot straight up like an Apollo missile launch. I strained and strained . . . my lungs felt like they wanted to burst . . . could I . . . could I . . .

I did see my whole life passing in front of me. I thought back to those childhood days when I slashed tree limbs out in the woods, driving Daddy's pickup truck, and then I imagined Marilyn sitting on the beach. I felt sorry that I was making her a widow in just our first week of marriage . . . when I suddenly popped above the ocean surface and gulped for air. To this day, I have no idea of how I survived that frightening experience.

I swam over to the inner tube holding the generator, panting for all I was worth.

"What happened?" Mike asked, intensely concerned.

"I don't know what happened. All I did was touch my nose."

"Well, I told you that you couldn't do that. Do you think you can swim over to that rock?"

"I think I can make it, but I have to swim slow."

We rested for about twenty minutes until I felt my strength coming back. Then we dog-paddled to shore. I remember walking out of the water, totally exhausted, and flopping myself down next to Marilyn. But I did not tell her what had happened or how I had cheated death that afternoon for at least a year because I didn't want to upset her.

Sitting on a beach towel that afternoon, I couldn't stop my hands from shaking. I had almost died at a time when life couldn't get much better. I had married the woman of my dreams, I had a No. 1 record, and money was pouring into my bank account. My thoughts, though, turned to God, whom I hadn't thought about in a long time. As I watched the brilliant orange sun dip toward the horizon, I wondered what it all meant. My guess was that God decided it wasn't my time yet.

If there was one thing I had learned about life and about music, it was all about timing.

"People were just ready

for a new sound,

and the new sound in the

early Seventies was

more real and edgy."

CHAPTER 8

ONE LESS BELL TO ANSWER

I don't know how in the world
to stop thinking of him . . .

Marilyn: Our album *The Age of Aquarius* turned out to be a monster hit—selling in the millions, with the single later winning us our fifth and sixth Grammys, including our second Record of the Year. The thought that millions of people around the world had purchased "Aquarius" and were singing "along with the 5th Dimension" sent shivers up our collective spines.

We could suddenly play any house—including the White House. In late 1969, we were invited to sing at 1600 Pennsylvania Avenue, which was an incredible honor for the group. Trumpeter Al Hirt and the 5th Dimension performed at a private concert in the East Room before all fifty US governors and their wives, plus the Most Powerful Man in the Free World—President Richard Nixon, and his wife, Pat, who sat in the front row. It was hard not to get all caught up in the atmosphere of the historic White House, but we wanted to put on a good show.

A funny thing—or strange thing—happened prior to our appearance. A White House aide sent us a questionnaire, which included a question asking if any of our lyrics referred to drugs or taking drugs. When we asked for a clarification, the White House aide told us that they were interested in a particular song of ours called "Up, Up and Away." Since cocaine was sold in "balloons," or packages, he said, was there a hidden meaning behind "Up, Up and Away"? We replied that it was just a happy song about the joys of riding in a hot air balloon.

Billy: During our White House concert, Marilyn said she was too nervous to sneak a look at President Nixon, but I did. I noticed he was bobbing his head to our music—and I'm not going to comment on whether he had the beat right. We did take a risk by performing a song called "The Declaration," which was part of a medley that included "A Change Is Gonna Come" and "People Got to Be Free." The medley started with us singing the Declaration of Independence set to music:

> We hold these truths to be self-evident, that all men are created equal, that they are endowed by their Creator with certain unalienable Rights, that among these are Life, Liberty and the pursuit of Happiness. That to secure these rights, Governments are instituted among Men, deriving their just powers from the consent of the governed, that whenever any Form of Government becomes destructive of these ends, it is the Right of the People to alter or to abolish it, and to institute new Government, laying its foundation on such principles and organizing its powers in such form, as to them shall seem most likely to effect their Safety and Happiness. Prudence, indeed, will dictate that Governments long established should not be changed for light and transient causes; and accordingly all experience hath shewn, that mankind are more disposed to suffer, while evils are sufferable, than to right

themselves by abolishing the forms to which they are accustomed. But when a long train of abuses and usurpations, pursuing invariably the same Object evinces a design to reduce them under absolute Despotism, it is their right, it is their duty, to throw off such Government, and to provide new Guards for the future security.

Performing that three-part song was our little protest, a political statement, if you will. If President Nixon was listening closely, he would have heard us sing that when the government becomes destructive of unalienable rights, the people have the right to institute a new government. We weren't exactly John, Paul, George, and Ringo singing, "You say you want a revolution," but we were definitely pushing the boundaries.

The weirdest thing happened when we finished "The Declaration." The East Room fell totally silent! There was a long, awkward moment as the US governors and their wives waited to gauge President Nixon's reaction.

I froze in my tracks for several seconds, waiting . . . waiting . . . until President Nixon stood up and clapped his hands. Within seconds, the East Room filled to the rafters with applause. I made eye contact with Marilyn and winked as we bowed, but let me tell you, that was the most nervous moment I've ever had on stage.

Afterward, President Nixon met with us, and he brought along his wife and daughter Tricia. He appeared to be cool, and he didn't say anything about "The Declaration" while the White House cameraman took pictures for posterity.

Marilyn: Yes, there were some nervous moments, but we encountered some unexpected controversy *afterward* when we were criticized in some quarters for "selling out" or losing our "soulful edge" by singing in the Nixon White House, but we never saw it that way. Whenever the President of the United States asks you to come into the nation's most famous residence to perform, you go. It's like a command performance. We were entertainers, which meant we checked our politics at the front door of the White House. If truth be told, we didn't vote for Nixon (we came from families of lifelong Democrats), but that was beside the point.

While singing in the White House was a prestigious honor, probably the biggest concert billing that we were part of happened on June 13, 1971, when the 5th Dimension were invited to perform at the 50th Anniversary Celebration for the Motion Picture and Television Relief Fund.

Now, I can tell there's some head-scratching going on. *What's the Motion Picture and Television Relief Fund?* The Relief Fund provided medical, dental, and financial help to Hollywood industry members, and what a gala event that was, held at the Dorothy Chandler Pavilion in Los Angeles!

The honored guest was HSH Princess Grace of Monaco (HSH stands for Her Serene Highness), and the entertainment program featured this all-star lineup:

- Jimmy Durante

- Mitzi Gaynor

- Bob Hope and the Golddiggers

- Pearl Bailey, backed by a cancan team of "dancers" that included Sammy Davis, Jr., Rock Hudson, Jack Lemmon, Joe Namath, David Niven, and Don Rickles.

After the intermission, the 5th Dimension took the stage, and we were followed by Jack Benny, Barbra Streisand, and Frank Sinatra. This was billed as Frank's "farewell" performance. (Frank's "farewell performances" would continue more than fifteen years.)

Oh, and did I mention that Cary Grant and James Stewart made the introductions?

When I walked out on stage, the first person I saw was actor Edward G. Robinson sitting in the front row, and I said to myself, *Oh, no, what have I gotten myself into here?*

Whenever I performed in public I usually experienced preconcert jitters, but nothing approached the stage fright that gripped my throat on that star-studded evening. I was very nervous. I think our third song was "One Less Bell to Answer," which was my solo—and my turn in the spotlight. When I started singing a song I had sung a hundred times before, I had no idea where my voice was. All I knew was that my throat was trembling like a schoolgirl's first recital. I somehow managed to finish the song without keeling over from nervousness.

My second-worst onstage experience had happened a couple of years earlier in Munich, West Germany, with Omar Sharif, Sophia Loren, and German actress Senta Berger watching from the front rows. In those days, German fans threw flowers to show their appreciation, and in the middle of one energetic song, I kicked one leg high in the air while my support leg landed on a flower, causing that leg to slip out from underneath me.

Billy: When I turned around and saw Marilyn, both legs were up in the air—and the only thing that was going to hit the ground was her you-know-what.

I said to myself, *Oh, I can't watch this.* Marilyn hit the floor so hard that it scared me, but before I knew it, she bounced right back up and got back in step.

When the number was over, I came over to her and whispered, "What happened?" because I knew she had hurt herself.

Marilyn: For me, everything happened in slow motion while I was flipped into the air. *Oh no, I'm going to fall flat on my butt in front of all these people.* I didn't know whether to milk this for all that it was worth, or get up and continue on. In a split second I decided to jump right back up—even as I was in midair—and hope that not too many people would notice.

Oh, was I hurting. I hurt for about a year before I went to the doctor and found out that I had chipped my tailbone. Not much could be done except live with the pain.

I also had to live with the marriage I made. The arguing that was a hallmark of our living-together relationship followed us right into the early years of our marriage. We argued about what was the best way to beat the LA traffic, especially on the way to LAX, which had about five different routes on surface streets. We sparred on how things got done around the house. One time, Billy came into the kitchen, where I was heating up some leftovers on the stove. "Isn't that flame a little too high?" he asked.

I glared at him. "Who's doing the cooking here?" I replied sharply.

Billy drove me nuts when he took a shower because he put his wet towel on the doorknob every time. "Can't you put it on the rack?" I demanded. Another pet peeve of mine was when he put his drinking glass on our wooden furniture without a protective coaster.

I was on a one-woman mission to change Billy. In my mind, he needed to be told how to act, what to say, and what to wear. Couldn't Billy see that he was doing everything wrong?

Billy: If there was an easy way to get things done, Marilyn would always find the hard way. She was wound way too tight, and I didn't like the way she talked down to me when we talked about business. I was bugged when she would listen to the people directing our careers and take their opinions as the gospel truth instead of listening to my ideas. But when it came to major decisions affecting our lives, we always found a way to work out our differences. We would discuss—often argue about—our viewpoints until we arrived at a conclusion that made sense to both of us. We always tried to see the big picture.

An example of a challenge that I had to work through was when the record company floated the idea of releasing the 5th Dimension's first song featuring a solo, rather than a group singing effort that had been our signature since "Go Where You Wanna Go."

There was a little history to be dealt with. In 1967, we had recorded a song on *The Magic Garden* album called "The Worst That Could Happen" with me singing the lead. A lot of people slapped me on the back and said I did a great job, which prompted talk of releasing "The Worst That Could Happen" as a single. Johnny Rivers and Soul City Records, however, took the position that the 5th Dimension sound was a group sound, and no singles would be released unless the entire group was singing the vocals. That made sense to me, I guess. Today, that would be called "branding," and the 5th Dimension did have a unique pop sound.

Well, guess what? A group called the Brooklyn Bridge heard my version of "The Worst That Could Happen," and—shades of the Johnny Mann Singers and "Up, Up and Away"—they covered my song and put it out as a single!

So what's the worst that could happen to a song called "The Worst That Could Happen"? How about going all the way to No. 1? I couldn't believe it. My hit hitting the top of the charts. That was a kick in the teeth to me. To add insult to injury, the Brooklyn Bridge version sounded so much like me that my family back in St. Louis, Marilyn, and even I thought I was the one singing.

Flash forward two years, and Bones Howe and the record company executives were considering the release of another single following "Aquarius." It's not my intention to brag here, but we were hot after having a No. 1 hit sit on top of the charts for six weeks. This was the time to strike again while the world was listening to us.

Marilyn: I know where Billy is going with this. One night while we were working on various cuts for the *Age of Aquarius* album, Bones Howe approached me with a sly grin on his face. "Check these lyrics out," he said, handing me a typewritten sheet.

Bill, I love you so, I always will
I look at you and see the passion eyes of May
But am I ever gonna see my wedding day?
Oh, I was on your side Bill
When you were losin'
I'd never scheme or lie Bill
There's been no foolin'
But kisses and love won't carry me
Till you marry me Bill

This was *before* Billy's marriage proposal to me and during the period when Mommy was asking me if Billy was going to make an honest woman out of me. "That's cute, Bones," I said.

"It would be really funny if you did this song as a joke on the album," he said. "It's a solo, you know."

Now I was interested. "What's the arrangement like?" I asked.

"Oh, you'll like it," he said. "Laura Nyro wrote it and put it on her debut album, but it didn't go anywhere."

I was game. When I heard the tune, I was thrilled. I had wanted to sing torch songs since I was a little girl. At the same time, the irony of singing "but kisses and love won't carry me till you marry me Bill" didn't escape me. I definitely had my tongue firmly in cheek when I put on the headphones and sang in the studio, and it sounded like Laura had written "Wedding Bell Blues" after interviewing Billy and me. Was it a case of life imitating art or art imitating life?

So when Bones and the record company executives discussed a follow-up single to "Aquarius," they kept coming back to "Wedding Bell Blues."

When word got out that they were considering "Wedding Bell Blues" as a single, the other members of the group—including Billy—questioned the wisdom of releasing a solo. They asked Bones if we were changing our long-held policy of no solo singles. Billy said that he hadn't forgotten how he missed out on "The Worst That Could Happen."

Then Soul City Records heard that a San Diego radio station had jumped on "Wedding Bell Blues," giving it significant airplay. That sealed the deal in their minds. We released "Wedding Bell Blues" as a single, and their instincts proved correct. The first 5th Dimension solo shot up to No. 1 in the fall of 1969, giving us our second No. 1 hit that year.

Now we were *really* the toast of the town. If there is anything the entertainment industry respects, it's money, and we were raking it in for the record company. Liberty Records, the parent company of Soul City Records, ran a full-page advertisement in the *Wall Street Journal* picturing the 5th Dimension with the tagline "Their music hath charm—$14 million worth." Everything we sang turned to gold, and for a moment in time, we sat atop the pop universe.

People who remember us from that era sometimes ask us how and why the 5th Dimension became a pop phenomenon. This isn't the complete answer, but when you consider the tenor of the times—the late Sixties and early Seventies—you can see that the 5th Dimension was all about entertaining. We were not a protest act; we were about having good, clean fun. We came along at a time when the American society was experiencing upheaval and uncertainty, and young people were protesting the Vietnam War on college campuses and in the streets. And then we came along riding in our beautiful balloon, and we let a ray of sunshine into a dark period of our nation's history.

When the 5th Dimension was at its peak, the movie *Patton* was released and would later win the Oscar for Best Picture in 1970. The film starred George C. Scott as the controversial, multidimensional, and heroic World War II general. Toward the end of the movie, Patton was shown riding into the sunset, telling the story of how Roman generals came home from their wars with their defeated enemies marching in front of them, all in chains. While boisterous crowds cheered the victorious Roman general's name as he rode his chariot majestically into Rome, a humble man stood alongside the general, whispering, "Remember, all fame is fleeting."

Looking back through the prism of time, I wish somebody had been whispering the same thing into our ears. Not because we didn't appreciate the rewards that success brought us, because we did and we have. We *loved* every minute in the sun—and our fame lasted a lot longer than Andy Warhol's proverbial "fifteen minutes." When we sang *let the sun shiiiine in* before sold-out audiences from Portland, Oregon, to Portland, Maine, we could definitely feel the warmth of applause that seemed to wrap around us like a woolen shawl.

Our status as one of the top pop groups led to our most interesting foreign tour in the spring of 1973 when the 5th Dimension toured Turkey and Eastern Europe under a United States Cultural Presentations Program sponsored by the US Department of State. Only our expenses were covered; we waived our performance fees to be part of this special "cultural exchange" program and canceled domestic engagements to perform and participate in various "goodwill" workshops in Turkey, Poland, Romania, and Czechoslovakia.

Remember, this was the height of the Cold War days, and the Iron Curtain separated the repressed Soviet-bloc countries from free, democratic Western countries.

Billy: Turkey was the most fascinating country for me, although it was like going back in time. I found out where all our old cars go. They were belching exhaust, and the air was filthy. But I didn't dwell on that because this was a time to learn what was happening in different cultures. I loved walking through the Grand Bazaar in Istanbul—the outdoor market where vendors set out their wares—and seeing what they offered. Let me tell you, it was a startling sight to see our albums for sale in a Turkish bazaar. They looked like our albums, but it didn't take more than a quick glance to know that they were "bootleg" copies. We asked where they got them, but all they wanted us to do was autograph their bootleg copies!

Maybe I should have purchased a copy as a souvenir, but what I did buy was a very nice gold bracelet for Marilyn as a memento of the trip. I also thought the famous Blue Mosque was an interesting sight.

Then we hopped a short flight from Istanbul to Bucharest. We had around fifteen people with us—our manager Marc Gordon, a road manager, a sound man, several musicians, and a few roadies, including a lighting guy who was a loud, flamboyant character. As we passed through immigrations and customs, everyone became very quiet as we watched the border guards rip open our luggage and rummage through our belongings.

Our wardrobe trunk must have looked suspicious because they tore into it with a crowbar and really wrecked it. Eventually, nothing of interest was found, and when we got back on our bus, our interpreter told us that since our flight had come from Turkey, they were looking for hashish or other types of drugs.

The movie *Midnight Express*, about an American thrown into a Turkish prison for drug smuggling, wouldn't be released until 1978, but when I saw Brad Davis's portrayal, I shivered. Not because we had any drugs that day in Bucharest, but if someone in the band had done something really stupid . . . or someone had planted some hash . . .

The State Department had warned us in no uncertain terms that we could not have any drugs with us, and if we did, they could not help us. They didn't need to worry.

Marilyn: Once we got that incident at the Bucharest airport behind us, traveling behind the Iron Curtain was a trip. Our entire time I felt like we were the only black people in these countries. In many places, adults—and especially the children—would stare at us as though they had never seen any people of color before. They probably hadn't.

A young woman was our interpreter, and she was fascinated with us. There would be times when she would be sitting in the dressing room with Florence and me, and she would be asking us questions about life in the United States when suddenly she would stop talking and turn away from us, as if we hadn't been talking. Florence and I would look at each other because we thought this was rude, ill-mannered behavior. Then we realized that she did this every time a guy in a gray suit walked by.

Our interpreter in Bucharest had some outrageous ideas about life in the United States. She had heard that all Americans carried guns on their hips, just like the cowboys did a hundred years ago. She thought everyone took drugs and lived in big, expensive apartments, but she was believing only what she had been told by the Communist government.

Since Bucharest was our first stop behind the Iron Curtain, we had to get used to being followed. In Bratislava, Czechoslovakia, Billy, Ronald, and I enjoyed eating out at a hotel close to where we were staying. When we decided to walk back to our hotel after our meal, we could immediately tell that two guys were tailing us. We got a bit scared because we didn't know who they were, so we started walking faster. They started walking faster. We didn't know what they wanted, so we made a big circle back to our hotel, where we stopped in front of the lobby and refused to go any farther. The two men realized what we were doing and walked by us.

When we came home from our trip, the 5th Dimension was invited to appear on the CBS Sunday morning show *Face the Nation*, to discuss in serious tones what we saw and learned about life behind the Iron Curtain. That was unusual because I don't think any pop music groups had been asked to appear on a network news program before to discuss world affairs.

Those were some of the wonderful times we had as part of the 5th Dimension. Following our Eastern Europe trip, we hit a period where music started changing, and our music wasn't being requested as it had been, which is a nice way of saying that we weren't selling as many records.

We first noticed the slowdown in sales after the release of "(Last Night) I Didn't Get to Sleep," which sold a million copies and reached No. 8 on the charts. Our next single, "If I Could Reach You," sold half as many copies, and no one seemed to be talking about what a happening act the 5th Dimension were. Our signature smooth harmonies that had thrilled audiences for seven years were no longer moving them as they had before. People were just ready for a new sound, and the new sound in the early Seventies was more real and edgy.

We heard that everyone has their run in the popular music entertainment industry. Everyone has their shelf life. When record sales don't approach the huge numbers as they did in the past, it's hard to accept and difficult to deal with. I found it hard to imagine that we would not have any more hits when we had so many in the past. We came to expect them. Not that everything we put out there became a hit with the public, but our batting average was pretty darn good.

Just like the nose of a jet airplane making a nearly minute shift that starts the long descent, the 5th Dimension had to face a new reality: Music was changing, and our sound was not part of that change.

Billy: I felt we shouldn't stand by idly while the pop scene passed us by. I lobbied for changing the group's sound and trying something new because the old ways weren't working any longer. Marilyn was in my corner, but the others weren't. Ronald said our group sound was what made us famous, so we should stay with it.

We recorded two more unsuccessful albums—in 1974 (*Soul and Inspiration*) and 1975 (*Earthbound*)—and they were not pleasant experiences for any of us, including the latter album, which reunited the group with songwriter Jimmy Webb. We were having more and more tension-filled disagreements and conflicts about the future of the 5th Dimension.

When the *Earthbound* master was sent to us for final review, Marilyn and I listened to it. We did not like what we heard. I'll never forget Marilyn saying to me, "I don't know how I can do another album with the group. This was so difficult, and I'm not pleased with the result."

"Maybe it's time for us to leave the group," I said.

"This is hard for me to say,

but I have to say it:

Marilyn and I have

decided to leave the group

and move on."

CHAPTER 9

YOU DON'T HAVE TO BE A STAR
(TO BE IN MY SHOW)

*There'll be no cheering from the crowds,
just two hearts beating out loud . . .*

Marilyn: After the *Earthbound* experience, we realized the spark was definitely gone for us. Billy was the first to talk about leaving the 5th Dimension. I can remember him shaking his head and saying to me, "I don't know if I can do this any longer. Maybe it's time for a change."

I knew he felt strongly about it. While hits were getting harder to come by, it wasn't *that* long ago that we had been popular, but the record-buying public had moved on. Maybe there was something we could all do to turn the 5th Dimension around, but we both wanted to see what else was out there for us. Billy and I never lost the dream of becoming solo artists, and the timing seemed right. I was in my early thirties, Billy was in his mid-thirties, and our vocal chops were at their strongest. Could we make it as solo acts? Being the captain of our own ships had its appeal, and we were both independent-minded enough to leave safe harbor and chart a new course on pop music's open seas.

Nonetheless, this was a *huge* career move that needed some level-headed thinking. We would be leaving a family of three close friends with whom we had shared some incredibly exciting years, and we had grown to depend on one another. We would be splitting from a group that was still earning handsome amounts of money, and while our record sales had dipped, we still had legions of fans buying our albums and coming out to see us perform. Even if we were dropped by our record label (which we weren't), we could still perform in smaller venues and make a nice living singing "Up, Up and Away" and "Aquarius/Let the Sun Shine In" till the cows came home. But we weren't ready to rest on our laurels. We believed there were new roads to travel, new records to make, and maybe there would be more Grammys in our future. So painfully we decided to leave the 5th Dimension.

Billy: Leaving the group was our decision. No one suggested it or pushed us in that direction, and sadly Florence, Ronald, and Lamonte never saw it coming. We thought about the right time to deliver the bad news, figuring our departures would upset them deeply. We decided to tell them in June 1975 at the end of our weeklong engagement at the Westbury Music Fair in Long Island, New York. We knew when this gig was over, everyone would be taking a short vacation before the start of the busy summer season, so this would give them time to digest the news.

As we got closer to the day of reckoning, Marilyn got cold feet. I said to her, "Baby, I'll tell you what. Why don't you stay with the group and let me go out there and see what happens for me?"

She thought about that statement for about five minutes before replying, "I don't want to be in the 5th Dimension if you're not part of it."

After our performance—a matinee—we asked the rest of the group, along with Marc Gordon, our manager, to meet us back at the hotel. When

I had everyone's attention, I cleared my throat and spoke up, knowing this wouldn't be easy.

"This is hard for me to say, but I have to say it: Marilyn and I have decided to leave the group and move on." I looked over and saw Marilyn in tears.

The rest of the group was stunned, but as the reality settled in over the next few weeks, their surprise turned to hurt and anger—and understandably so. Marilyn and I were changing their lives, and they felt betrayed. What began as a lark in 1965—when Lamonte suggested we do some group singing—had become our identities as performers and, to some extent, as people. When you live, travel, perform, and promote as a fivesome for a decade, you become a family in many ways. We loved each other. We had gone through a lot together, and the highs always outweighed the lows.

We agreed to stay with the 5th Dimension for another five months to fulfill our contract obligations to perform at various venues and give Florence, Ronald, and Lamonte time to find replacements. We tried to make it as easy as possible for them to continue performing as the 5th Dimension. We walked away from everything: the name, the clothes, the music, and the record deal. All we wanted from them was love and understanding; it took years to achieve that.

That summer, Ronald got sick and had to stay home, so it was just the four of us out there. We always wondered if the stress had an impact on his health. But Marilyn and I were committed to ending our participation on as high a note as we could. There were hurt feelings on all sides, and the tension kept growing. Our final concert with the 5th Dimension happened at the Rivera Hotel in Las Vegas on November 5, 1975.

Shortly before our engagement, we met a couple of times with Marc. He said he understood why I wanted to see what was out there for me, but then he turned to Marilyn and held out an olive branch to her. "If you want the security of staying with the group, you can do that," he said, but Marilyn shook her head no.

Marilyn: Marc approached us on our last night in Las Vegas and said there would be no farewell party because the group wasn't ready to acknowledge our departure to the public. They felt that it would be better to keep things quiet until they could announce the new group members. "I hope that's all right," he said.

"It's not all right," Billy replied for the both of us. We felt that with all the people who had come to see our final performance—family members, friends, and people who had played important roles in the success of the 5th Dimension—that some kind of closure should take place. It would be healing for everybody.

Marc decided at the last minute to hold a farewell reception for us in one of the Riviera's suites. When we walked in that night, the room temperature felt as chilly as the cold November winds whipping off the Nevada desert. Maybe this wasn't a good idea after all. All of us wandered around in a daze. Florence didn't mingle much, but was engrossed in a serious conversation with our friend Sonny Porter. Ronald looked sad, and Lamonte laughed and circulated among the guests, but without his usual flair. We were all reeling from the knowledge that everything was going to change. Billy and I were afraid to think about what the future would bring. When we said our good-byes, we felt a sadness that only time could heal.

The hard feelings were unfortunate, but we had decided to move on. At that time, the 5th Dimension's label was ABC Records, owned by the same company that owned the ABC television network. Billy and I met with Jerry Rubenstein, the president, and when he heard we were leaving the group to pursue solo careers, he said that we had a home with ABC Records.

I got into the studio and recorded some solo efforts, and Billy did the same. We were ready to be up, up, and on our way, but then we started to rethink this direction. Separate singing careers meant separate tours. We could go for months without seeing each other. What would happen to our relationship if I got a hit and Billy didn't? How would I react if my songs fizzled and Billy's hit record put him on the cover of *People* magazine with the headline "Pop's Latest Sex Symbol"? Something like that could mess up a marriage.

Billy and I started having "what if" conversations—what if we sang together as a duet? As exciting as the possibility of solo careers sounded to us, the thought of not doing it together was something we didn't want to do. Besides, we joked to each other, who would we argue with? Billy said he didn't want to go back to arguing with the empty seat next to him on the tour bus.

We approached Jerry Rubenstein and explained our dilemma. Solo careers could hurt our marriage, we said, and our marriage was worth more than individual success. We asked whether we could perform as "Marilyn McCoo and Billy Davis, Jr." and release albums featuring the both of us.

Jerry liked the idea of a husband-and-wife act, and there were several popular ones at the time. Sonny and Cher were starring in a successful variety television show, trading quips about their divorce. The Captain and Tennille—comprised of the husband-and-wife team of Daryl Dragon and Toni Tennille—had just seen their huge hit "Love Will Keep Us Together" win the Grammy for Record of the Year. They, too, had their own variety show on the ABC network. Another married couple, Nick Ashford and Valerie Simpson, wrote "Ain't No Mountain High Enough" for Diana Ross and had their own successful recording career.

I had been working with producer Don Davis on my solo songs, and I liked his work, so it seemed a natural fit when Otis Smith, head of A&R

at ABC Records, suggested that Don work with Billy and me on our first album, which was called *I Hope We Get to Love in Time.*

We released the title track as a single, but it failed to catch on. No problem. We had high hopes for the second single—a song called "You Don't Have to Be a Star (to Be in My Show)." The song had a catchy, pop feel that made you feel good in an "Up, Up and Away" type of way. We took turns singing this duet:

Baby, come as you are with just your heart and I'll take you in.
You're rejected and hurt, to me you're worth what you have within.
Now I don't need no superstar 'cause I'll accept you as you are.
You won't be denied because I'm satisfied with the love you inspire.
You don't have to be a star, baby, to be in my show.
You don't have to be a star, baby, to be in my show.

"You Don't Have to Be a Star" rocketed to No. 1 on the Billboard Top 40—and later won a Grammy for "Best Rhythm and Blues Vocal Performance by a Duo, Group or Chorus." To reach this level of success so soon after our departure from the 5th Dimension astounded Billy and me.

Professionally, and personally to some extent, it felt great to be back on top of the pop world with other great acts—Diana Ross, Hall & Oates, Elton John, Tony Orlando and Dawn, Abba, John Denver, the Carpenters, and the Bee Gees. We were making a lot more money now. The world was our oyster, and like George and Louise Jefferson in a popular TV sitcom at the time (*The Jeffersons*), we were "moving on up" in more ways than one.

Now, there's something you need to know about our houses. When Billy and I got married, we purchased our first home in 1969 in the Valley—San Fernando Valley. Our home in Sherman Oaks was located on a nice cul-de-sac perched on the hillside with a stunning view of the . . . San Diego Freeway, but if you liked a view that changed all the time, then this was your house. At night, the headlights and taillights of thousands of cars stretched out like a red-and-white necklace sitting atop a blanket of black velvet. My mother loved sitting behind our picture window and watching the traffic pass by.

Several years later, we moved into a striking home in nearby Encino situated on nearly two acres with a main house, a guesthouse, and a swimming pool and tennis court in the backyard. We lost our freeway view, however. When Billy and I left the 5th Dimension and had a No. 1 hit right away, we thought about making another move. But first, a little geography lesson here.

Separating the San Fernando Valley and the Los Angeles city proper is a series of hills, including a very famous series of foothills called Beverly Hills.

Beverly Hills. Its very name is synonymous with wealth and success, and the elite of the entertainment world and captains of industry lived behind the sandstone walls surrounding their magnificent mansions. Billy and I loved being invited to lavish parties where the rich and famous mingled in their formal wear and expensive jewelry, clinking glasses filled with Dom Perignon champagne and snacking on caviar canapés and wedges of Camembert cheese. The presence of paparazzi snapping their flash pictures only heightened the excitement of these glittering affairs.

Sure, we knew that some of these rich and successful people walked around with their noses in the air, and some undoubtedly looked down upon anyone from "the Valley." But we also found many of these wealthy and successful folks to be very cordial to Billy and me, probably because they viewed us as peers in the rich and famous department.

With the success of "You Don't Have to Be a Star" adding more wealth to our net worth, Billy and I began talking about moving to Beverly Hills.

We drove around a few neighborhoods to get a feel for what we liked, and then we contacted a Realtor to show us a few houses—ah, mansions.

That first day, we walked through a wonderful eight-thousand-square-foot English Tudor estate built in the 1930s by famed architect Paul Williams. The home came with five bedrooms, five bathrooms, five fireplaces, maid's quarters, and a separate guest apartment over the garage. The mansion included a wonderful patio and swing set, and the upper terrace overlooked a backyard with a tennis court and a pool set inside a well-manicured garden.

We both fell immediately in love with this house. A British feel oozed charm from its slanted wood shake roof and small-paned, hand-cut windows to its half-timbered Elizabethan-style indoors with stained timbers and dark wooden trim. "That's the one I want," I announced to Billy, who loved this house as much as I did.

We purchased our dream home and immediately embarked on the fun chore of filling this mansion with "stuff"—items and souvenirs that we had collected while performing around the world, gold records and Grammys, and tasteful antique furniture to fit the feel of such a countrified "manor." We filled our closets with furs and the latest fashions and our walls with artwork. Inside the garage were two late-model cars—a Rolls Royce Corniche and a Mercedes 450 SLC.

The only thing missing was . . . a brother or sister for Steven. Billy and I had tried to conceive for years, but I just couldn't get pregnant. When my song "Wedding Bell Blues" climbed to No. 1 in the fall of 1969, I had to leave the group for two months to deal with some "female problems". Fibroids—which are tumors, usually benign—had developed inside my uterus. My doctor decided that the best course of action would be to cut them away from the uterine wall since they could affect the ability of a fertilized egg to develop. I submitted to this invasive cleanup surgery, but while I recuperated for six weeks, the group was on the road and Florence was singing my solo—and getting standing ovations!

As months turned into years of infertility, we sought out a fertility clinic for some answers, but we could never get pregnant. The pain of infertility was so deep that when writers and reporters probed on whether Billy and I would have children together, I deflected the question by saying that Billy and I were too busy and too committed to our careers with the 5th Dimension to have other children.

I don't know how I would have handled raising a newborn while trying to maintain a singing career. On one hand, I greatly desired giving birth to a child, but on the other hand, I had bought into this new thing called "women's lib," a social movement that began in the late Sixties, which said that women did not have to be mothers to be complete. This was a time when women—single or married—began referring themselves as "Ms."

Women were seeking equal pay for equal work and the same opportunity as men to succeed in the workplace and elsewhere in society, including the entertainment industry. I loved it when Billie Jean King dusted Bobby Riggs in that famous "Battle of the Sexes" tennis match in September 1973 before millions watching on TV. Billy and I started playing tennis during the tennis boom of the early Seventies, so I cheered mightily when the "libber" beat the "lobber."

I was also heavily influenced by a book I read called *The Female Eunuch* by Germaine Greer, a groundbreaking manifesto that portrayed marriage as a legalized form of slavery for women and attacked the systematic denial of women's rights by a male-dominated society. I didn't buy into everything that Germaine Greer wrote, however, which is why I felt conflicted about what my role should be as a wife and hope-to-be mother. I wanted a child—or two—in the worst way. We kept trying until 1979, when my "female problems" reached a point where the doctor recommended that I have a hysterectomy. The surgical procedure ended my dreams of bringing a new life into this world.

But I am a mother. Steven, Billy's son from his first marriage, had been spending time with us ever since we married in 1969, when he was five years old. Steven lived with his mother, now in Detroit, but every summer he came out West to vacation with us for several weeks. When Steven was eight, he asked if he could live with us year-round, and everyone agreed with this idea since Steven could spend more time with his father and enroll in better schools. We purchased the Encino home after he began living with us because we wanted more space for him.

Billy and I knew that having Steven under our roof meant that we would need some help raising him and caring for him when we were on the road. One of those live-in housekeepers, a lovely woman named Marge, keeled over and died of a heart attack in Steven's presence while we were in Omaha. That was a traumatic experience for everyone, especially Steven, but our housekeeper situation stabilized soon after when we hired a delightful British woman, Lilian Hawkins, to live with us and care for Steven. She had a warmth about her but a no-nonsense attitude that Steven needed, and Lilian became a part of the family. Every once in a while, she'd have a nip with Billy. She lived with us for ten years and really cared about Steven and, on occasion, looked after our two nieces, Mpambo and Dawn.

Billy: We needed a steady presence at home, especially as Marilyn and I became busy following the hit "You Don't Have to Be a Star." In June 1977, Marilyn and I were invited to participate in the Tokyo Music Festival, a major international event featuring entertainers from thirteen countries competing for recognition and awards. What made the trip extra special was taking Steven and Lilian with us to Japan.

We won the grand prize with a song called "The Two of Us," collecting three million yen, which sounded like a lot of money to us until we found out three million yen converted into $10,000. Still, the international exposure was nice, and we were asked to record "You Don't Have to Be a Star" in Japanese, which was a kick because we didn't know *what* we were singing as we phonetically sang the Japanese words.

When we came home from Tokyo, a new opportunity fell at our feet: television. CBS asked us to do a variety show during the summer of 1977—one of those famous "summer replacement" shows that networks put out there. Variety shows were popular television fodder during the 1970s. The networks felt that if you slapped together a big-name star or two, wrote a few good jokes, added a dash of flash, and performed a few hot numbers, you had a hit on your hands.

If our show caught on that summer, we would have become part of the new fall schedule. If the Nielsen numbers were nil, we knew we were history. *The Marilyn McCoo & Billy Davis, Jr. Show* debuted with Marilyn and me singing and performing comedy sketches.

Marilyn: Doing TV was a weird experience. When you're doing it for the first time, you don't know if the jokes are good or bad or if the skits really work. We had people patting us on the back and telling us what we wanted to hear. They kept laughing at the jokes in rehearsal, but we forgot they wrote the jokes, not us.

We weren't surprised when CBS did not renew our contract after we completed six shows. That was fine with us. We learned some things about TV work: You have to learn the songs really fast, which means you don't have time to learn them very well before performing them in front of millions of people. The other thing we learned is that viewers can get tired of your act when they see you each week, which can hurt your live appearances. It's like eating a chocolate cream puff dessert after every meal.

One bit of TV trivia: We did skits each week with a trio of fresh-faced comedians breaking into the business: Jay Leno (*The Tonight Show*), Tim Reid (*WKRP in Cincinnati*), and Lewis Arquette (a talented character actor).

Billy: Following our CBS variety show experience, we recorded our second duet album. This time we went back into the studio with Frank Wilson, who had been a producer with Motown. We knew Frank from way back, and he had some nice runs with different acts, including the Supremes. While it was good to work with an old friend, there was something about Frank that was *different.*

The first time we gathered to start recording *The Two of Us*, Frank asked everyone to stop what they were doing so that he could pray that the Lord would bless the project.

Pray? That certainly sounded like something strange to me. I hadn't done any of that stuff since I was a young teen in St. Louis. Then Frank began praying before every recording session. Later, acquaintances told us that Frank had become a born-again Christian, which explained a lot of things. His wife, Bunny, would drop by the studio, and while they were a wonderful couple, it seemed like every time Marilyn and I had a conversation with them, they would talk about Jesus. That was becoming a turnoff. When we finished with the project, we saw them as little as possible.

We released a couple of singles from *The Two of Us*: "Look What You've Done to My Heart" and "My Reason to Be Is You," which were our favorites. These songs became hits in . . . Japan. We released four singles from our second album, and all failed to catch on with the US audience. They were listening to a hot sound called "disco," which was sweeping the country in 1977 following the release of the film *Saturday Night Fever*, starring John Travolta and the success of the disco soundtrack of the Bee Gees.

Everyone at the record label said disco was a bandwagon we had to jump on. When we went into the studio in 1978 to record our third album, *Marilyn and Billy*, the record company gave a cut called "Shine on Silver Moon" to a talented engineer named Johnny Luongo, who remixed it and turned the song into a disco record. If the Bee Gees were worried about losing record sales to us, they didn't have to worry long. "Shine on Silver Moon" never became a hit.

Marilyn: As we moved into 1979, we could really tell that things were slowing down. We weren't being booked into the same places that we had worked before. Sure, we were invited back to Las Vegas, but instead of headlining, we were opening for comedians like Shecky Green, Alan King, and Don Rickles. Instead of playing Pine Knob, a huge outdoor amphitheater near Detroit, we were booked into DB's, a nice club located inside a Hyatt Regency in suburban Dearborn. Instead of playing Red Rocks, a famed outdoor venue outside Denver, we were booked into the Turn of the Century, a nightclub in the Mile High City. Seemingly overnight, we had gone from concerts to clubs.

Columbia Records, who had purchased our recording contract from ABC Records, asked us to work with three different producers to get things turned around. We recorded four songs with each producer, but Billy and I could not agree with the record company on the best artistic direction to take. Then they asked us to work with a jazz producer, but we didn't want to go that route, so we agreed to disagree, and we asked to be released from Columbia Records.

I remember one record executive telling us that we were making a big mistake, but we cut ourselves adrift anyway.

Our recording careers were officially in the tank.

". . . I began to realize

that I could only identify

myself in terms of my

musical accomplishments."

CHAPTER 10

THE ME NOBODY KNOWS

He reaches the deepest part of me at
a time when I need him most . . .

Marilyn: As 1980 rang in a new decade, we struggled when the phone stopped ringing. Poof—we were tossed on the scrap heap of popular culture and discovered what it felt like to be treated as washed-up entertainers. We found out that no matter how high we had flown in our beautiful balloon, the gentle descent back to Earth was not fun.

Oh, we still got invited to those fancy Beverly Hills parties. Before, the paparazzi would rush up to us to take our picture. Now they ignored Billy and me while they stormed past us to shoot whoever was "hot"— exciting new artists like Donna Summer or Andy Gibb. We were yesterday's news, and I can remember the lump in my throat after we left many a star-studded event.

I was depressed by this sudden turn of events and brooded about how I had taken so much for granted. Didn't these paparazzi know that we were Grammy winners with nearly two dozen hit records to our credit? My active mind churned these snubs while I lay on my bed at home. I thought about how sad it was that people judged us strictly on whether we had a hit record on the charts.

What do I do with my life now? I wondered. All I ever wanted to do was sing. That was my passion, but I began to realize that I could only identify myself in terms of my musical accomplishments. Then I asked myself several hard questions:

- What do all your accomplishments really mean?

- Are you only the sum total of your success?

- Beyond all the things you have done, who are you?

Contemplating these questions was so painful that sometimes I had to drop the thoughts and return to them later.

I can remember Billy finding me in the master bedroom and asking, "What are you doing?"

"Thinking, that's all."

"Baby, you can't just sit around thinking. You need to find something to do with your time."

Billy was using his time to pursue other avenues in the entertainment world that had always interested him, including managing and producing new acts. He took several undiscovered artists into the studio and began producing their songs . . . on our nickel. If he could sign these new acts to a label, then we made money. If none of the acts caught on, however, we would lose out. Developing new talent was a crapshoot, but I had learned long ago that Billy liked to gamble.

In my down mood, I found it easy to criticize him, which led to more arguments between us. I questioned some of his choices of artists and declared that he was careless for using our money to bankroll these new acts. "You should concentrate on acts that have a chance of making it!" I huffed.

When he retorted that at least he was doing something with his life, I reminded him of some of his failed business efforts over the years.

Billy: There were more than a few. Once I invested in a medical supply company. I put a lot of money into it, not knowing that I would be competing against the big boys in distributing product. Doctors, I found out, weren't interested in leaving long-term relationships with their medical supply companies to go with a start-up. I wish I had known that going in.

Then I invested in a construction company that was doing what was called Section 8 housing—Los Angeles public housing tracts. We got contracts from the city to build these public housing apartment tracts, but we didn't know that the city didn't pay you until ninety to one hundred-and-twenty days after completion. We needed money to go on to the next job. We could never catch up, but we didn't know that going in.

Marilyn: All I could think about while I curled up on my bed was how empty I felt inside. I was puzzled that I could feel so hollow even though Billy and I had a good marriage, excellent health, financial security beyond our wildest dreams, and a certain measure of fame. Yet I *still* felt that something was terribly wrong about this situation, which I began calling a "void." The emptiness I felt became my deepest secret, and I disclosed it to no one, not even Billy. I knew something was missing in my life, but I couldn't put a finger on it.

I admitted to myself that I had been searching for a long time. Shortly after we left the 5th Dimension, my father hounded us to try transcendental meditation as a way to deal with the demands of our hectic duet schedule and the stress accompanying it. He felt that TM would level us out and give Billy and me peace.

One evening, we checked out the Self-Realization Center, an ashram on Sunset Boulevard. Someone whispered my very own "special" mantra into my ear, which I later learned was the same as Billy's and everyone else's in the room that night. I listened intently and tried to get up to speed with a new vocabulary. A white-robed swami informed us that transcendental meditation was a spontaneous, effortless march of the mind to its own unbounded essence. Through transcendental meditation, the mind unfolded its potential for unlimited transcendental awareness and unity consciousness where every possibility was naturally available to the conscious mind, or so they said. I could never find the center of my being, but at least I tried during my short-lived experiment with TM.

While we were with the group, René DeKnight, the 5th Dimension's musical director, told us about Swami Muktananda. "The swami is such a wonderful spiritual leader," René said. "He can lead you down the path of spiritual fulfillment."

We listened to the swami speak one night, but his message on the meaning of the universe left us cold. We were like, "Yes . . . and?"

Then René was on to a new spiritual tangent. "Marilyn, Billy, I've got this guy I want you to meet. You've got to go down and hear this man. You'll get a lot out of what he has to say."

"What's his name?" I asked.

"Werner Erhard. He does these weekend seminars called est—Erhard Seminar Training."

We didn't exactly flap our wings in excitement, but René was persistent because he thought Werner Erhard walked on water. He even got us to go after we learned that est took place over two weekends and cost $400 a person, a nice chunk of change in those days.

We listened to Werner say some things that we couldn't disagree with: We had to take responsibility for our own lives, nobody could change the outcome except for us, and the power to change was within everyone. This was part of the something he called "the human potential movement."

"Everything that happens to you, you have control over," Werner said. "You control your destiny, and you can make anything and everything happen in your life that you want to happen." Est appeared to be a grab bag of existential philosophy, motivational philosophy, and Zen Master philosophy that would raise our consciousness to new levels. During the seminar, we politely listened to testimonial after testimonial from those who said they no longer embraced the victim mentality.

One of the famous things about the est seminars is how they don't let you go to the bathroom. They would pack several hundred people into a hotel ballroom and tell you that you were not allowed to go on a bathroom break until the appointed time (like the lunch break). It was all designed to break down your defenses to their message.

Billy: Some people just got up and went to the restrooms anyway, but there were those who wanted to play the game, so they just let it go right there. The leaders would talk about those who left and say, "See, they don't have any control."

Marilyn: On the second weekend, they brought people on stage, where the est leaders yelled into their faces. I'm not sure what they were trying to prove, but it struck me as a bunch of nonsense. I could see that est depended on how mentally strong you were. Upon the completion of the est training, we were hit up to attend *more* seminars that would take us to the "next level"—for a fee, of course.

Following est, René's next idea was listening to a new spiritual guru— a channeler named "Lazarus." This time we weren't interested. René begged us to join him for an evening with Lazarus, pleading, "Just this once," so we relented. Lazarus turned out to be a middle-aged woman who said she could speak whatever the spirit Lazarus wanted her to say. We felt like there was a spirit involved, but it gave Billy and me the creeps.

Then one quiet afternoon in November 1980, I was opening the mail and noticed that we had received an invitation from Frank and Bunny Wilson. Frank, who had produced our second duet album, was being honored by his church with a dinner at a local hotel, and we were invited to come.

Our paths hadn't crossed for a couple of years. I thought Billy and I could show that we still cared for them by attending this special event. I RSVP'd with Bunny, saying, "Sure, Billy and I would love to come."

We arrived at the downtown hotel, and from the minute we stepped inside the ballroom, the people seemed warm and loving. They told us how much they appreciated seeing us, that it was good we were there, and how Frank and Bunny were grateful that we made the effort to come. Nobody asked us what we were doing. They might have wondered that, but it must not have mattered to them.

This is so great, I thought. *These people care about us as persons.* They didn't care if we were big stars or no longer big stars; they seemed genuinely happy to see us.

Billy: "Can you believe how wonderful these people are?" Marilyn asked me. "That's the way church people are," I replied, because I remembered it from years ago.

Marilyn: We thoroughly enjoyed our time that evening, especially with Frank and Bunny, who tempered their Jesus talk and focused on how we were doing. We talked about getting together . . . just the four of us . . . so I invited them over to the house for dinner.

Then we settled back and listened to the main speaker, Pastor E.V. Hill of Mount Zion Missionary Baptist, which was Frank's church. We expected him to say some nice things about Frank's involvement in the church, but Pastor Hill took the opportunity to rain down some fire and brimstone on the audience. He pointed to people sitting at their tables and thundered, "If you don't repent of your sins and ask Jesus Christ into your life, you're going to hell!" This was precisely the type of language that had turned me off to Christianity for years. I quietly whispered to Billy, "Can we leave?" The minute Pastor Hill finished his scorching sermon, we said our good-byes to Frank and Bunny and hightailed it out of there.

We still wanted this lovely couple over for dinner, though, and they came over to our home several weeks later. After the dessert dishes were cleared away, Billy said to Frank, "Hey, I want you to hear some product I've been working on with one of my acts." So they left the room to do their producers' thing while Bunny and I enjoyed a coffee at the dining room table. She started talking to me about Jesus again. *Oh, no. Here we go again,* I thought, but she threw me off balance when she said, "Marilyn, if you ever feel like there's a void in your life, that's the Lord telling you that you need Him."

When she used that term *void,* I involuntarily shivered. *How did she know that? That was exactly what I was experiencing—a void in my life, and I hadn't told anyone this.*

"Tell me about this void," I said with an air of curiosity.

"Well, it's this emptiness you feel in your heart. Nothing can fill it— hit records, Grammy awards, a home in Beverly Hills, famous friends, or expensive vacations. Your emptiness is a God-shaped vacuum, and it can only be filled by Jesus, the Prince of Peace and Lord of Lords."

I was dumbstruck how Bunny knew exactly what I was feeling. We must have talked for more than an hour before Frank and Billy rejoined us, and then we switched to another subject. But the next day, Bunny called and suggested that I read the Bible.

I had sat through est, tried transcendental meditation, and read books on life after death—the paranormal—and all sorts of New Age stuff, but reading the Bible? *That old thing?*

"I tried reading the Bible years ago," I told Bunny. "I couldn't make sense of it."

"Let me help you," she replied. "What you have to do before you read is pray and ask the Lord to reveal His meaning to you. Start with the gospel of John in the New Testament. I'll call you tomorrow and see how you're doing. You can ask me any questions you want."

The next morning I read several chapters, which prompted all kinds of questions for Bunny. I wondered what John meant when he said the "Word was made flesh" or what the Bread of Life was. Bunny was very good in explaining Scripture to me, but when I stumped her, she didn't try to speak circles around me. "I don't have an answer for that," she said. "I'll have to get back to you on that."

For two weeks, she walked me through the gospel of John, and I learned why Jesus—the Son of God—came on this Earth and subjected Himself to a brutal execution on our behalf. His death and resurrection meant that we would not perish but have eternal life with Him.

Bunny knew I was ready to give my heart to Jesus Christ, and I knew I was ready as well. On a December night in 1980 (I wish I could remember the exact date), during one of our conversations, Bunny asked me if I was ready to receive Jesus' gift of salvation. When I said yes, she asked me to repeat the following prayer:

Dear Jesus, I come to You right now . . . and admit that I am a sinner. I repent of my sins against You. I believe You died on the cross for my sins . . . and that You rose again three days later. I ask that You forgive me . . . and that You come into my life. Amen.

There wasn't a flash or kaboom. In fact, I hung up the phone with mixed feelings because I wasn't sure what I had done. Over the next few days, though, the void disappeared and something about me felt . . . different. I was afraid to tell Billy that I had prayed the Sinner's Prayer, however, because I feared causing problems in our marriage. Another reason is that for many years, I had been death on born-again Christians, and now I had become one of *them.*

Billy: I didn't know what was going on with Marilyn, but I definitely noticed her going around the house reading the Bible. That was very strange. I asked myself, *What's my wife doing with a Bible in her hand?* I had never seen that before. I knew we had a big Bible in the house, but we never opened it. It had sat in our library with an inch of dust on it until Marilyn picked it up.

This went on for a few days—her closing the door to our bedroom and reading her Bible quietly. I knew she was calling Bunny, and I figured that she was talking to her friend about the Lord. In my heart, I felt convicted because I'd been there before. I had grown up in the church. I had left the church to pursue my fame and fortune, but I had never shared my church days with Marilyn or talked to her about spiritual things because we were too busy chasing our music careers.

Since she wasn't going to church when we met in 1965, I wasn't going to spoil a great relationship by bringing up God. But now the Holy Spirit convicted me, and I started to look at the situation. My wife was getting into God's Word, but I had never even mentioned my spiritual roots with her. She knew I had sung with a gospel group back in St. Louis, but that was all.

I had to do something. This conviction in my heart was getting so deep because I knew way down it should have been me talking about the Lord to her. I should have been the one showing Marilyn the Bible or leading her to church or at least opening up the spiritual part of our relationship. That should have been the man's job, but I didn't say anything to her, even after I thought she had become a Christian.

Marilyn: Now I started praying for Billy to receive the Lord. I felt like we needed to be in this together, so I prayed that the Lord would open up an opportunity for Billy to come to Him. I mentioned this great desire in my heart to Frank and Bunny, and Frank said, "Well, I got a thing I'm doing at the Roxy Theater."

"What thing?" I inquired.

"It's called 'Jesus at the Roxy,' and it'll be in two weeks on Sunday night."

The Roxy was a revered rock 'n' roll club on Sunset Boulevard. For this special Sunday night program, Frank said he had asked several mainstream artists who were believers to lead an evening of song and testimonies: people like Philip Bailey from Earth, Wind, and Fire; Leon Patillo from Santana; Syreeta Wright, who sang with her former husband Stevie Wonder; and Deniece Williams, a rising recording artist who had also sung with Stevie Wonder. They would share their faith and talk about how the Lord changed their lives.

I immediately began plotting how to get Billy to "Jesus at the Roxy."

Billy: A few days before the event, I was driving along Sunset Boulevard with Marilyn. We came upon the Roxy Theater, and I spotted the marquee advertising "Jesus at the Roxy" on Sunday night. Marilyn exclaimed, "Oh, look, Baby, they're having 'Jesus at the Roxy.' That's one of Frank's projects. This could be fun. What do you think if we go?"

Remember, I had been feeling convicted about my lack of spiritual leadership, so I heard myself saying, "Sure, let's go; let's check it out."

When we arrived that evening, the place was packed. We found a table and took our seats. I enjoyed the music and hearing the testimonies from the Christian artists, and then Pastor Billy Ingram took the stage and preached out of the Bible. He finished by giving an altar call, asking whether anyone in the audience wanted to receive Jesus Christ into their hearts and know they would have eternal life with Him.

"With every head bowed and every eye closed, if you want to receive the Lord, please stand up," he said. "If you want to renew your relationship with the Lord, please stand up at your table." I sat there frozen to my seat, my head bowed and my eyes closed. I thought about how I had turned my back on the Lord all these years. I *knew* He was my Savior, but like the Prodigal Son who left his father's estate to chase after his own dreams, I walked away from the Lord. But now I could return. Now I could make a stand and be counted for Christ. I stood up because I knew it was my time, keeping my head bowed because I was thanking the Lord for receiving me into the kingdom.

Marilyn: I had been reading in the Bible where Jesus said, "If you confess me before men, then I will confess you before my Father who is in heaven." When Billy Ingram asked whether anyone wanted to come to Christ or renew his or her relationship with the Lord, I knew it was my time to stand and declare openly my decision to ask Jesus into my heart. My first prayer had been over the phone. I didn't know what Billy would do, but he would find out tonight that I was born again. When I stood up at my table, I couldn't resist the temptation to peek and see what Billy was up to. He was standing up!

Billy: I didn't know Marilyn was standing up until I opened my eyes after we finished praying with Pastor Ingram. That was such an unbelievable night! Marilyn and I rushed into each other's arms, and we both had tears running down our faces.

Marilyn: Bunny called me later in the week and said, "Well, now we have to find you a church and a Bible study to attend."

"Wait! This is too much too fast," I replied. "I didn't stand up for all that. I just wanted to get rid of the void. What's this Bible study and church all about?"

Bunny explained it beautifully to me. "When you have a new friend, somebody you really love and care about, and that someone really loves and cares about you, you want to know more about him, and you want to spend as much time with him as you can. It's the same way with Jesus. You have to become as little children, and children want to know about their daddies and the world around them."

Bunny pointed us toward an evening Bible study at Philip Bailey's house, which later moved to Donna Summer's office (Donna had become a Christian during the height of the disco craze). Frank and Bunny wanted us to go to their church, Mount Zion Missionary Baptist, but we liked the way Billy Ingram taught the Bible, so we began attending Maranatha Community Church in Inglewood.

Once Billy and I became Christians, *everything* changed. I no longer worried about our future because our lives were totally in His hands. Instead of dreading the dawning of a new day, I couldn't wait to see what the Lord had in store for Billy and me.

"We had decided

that this was a good

time to seek out

individual opportunities."

CHAPTER 11

MY
REASON TO BE
IS YOU

Now my life is alive,
my searching is through . . .

Marilyn: At the same time Billy and I were standing up at "Jesus at the Roxy," a new TV show was appearing on independent stations called *Solid Gold*. Dionne Warwick was the original host of this syndicated one-hour pop music program built around the Top 10 songs in the country. *Solid Gold* was a "hit parade" show that showcased a half-dozen up-and-coming acts while the *Solid Gold* dancers, dressed in skimpy and flashy costumes, "interpreted" the hit songs in the background.

After Dionne left the show, my agent received a phone call from the *Solid Gold* producers. They had signed Andy Gibb, a young heartthrob singer, to fill the opening, but now they wanted someone to share the hosting duties. Was I interested in auditioning for the cohost role?

Very much so. I had been exploring my solo aspirations in recent months for several reasons. We had decided that this was a good time to seek out individual opportunities. Billy was pursuing his business ventures, like marketing medical supplies. Coming to the Lord gave us confidence about the strength of our marriage, and Billy had given me his blessing to book solo engagements. I had found a personal manager, Sara Boyers, who was full of creative ideas to help guide me in this new, uncharted course for my career. Along with a gifted choreographer, Lester Wilson, we put together my new solo act with two male backup singer/dancers.

One of my first solo appearances was opening for Ben Vereen at John Ascuaga's Nugget casino in Reno, Nevada. I was *petrified* the first time I walked onstage. I looked around—no 5th Dimension, no Billy. I looked into the audience, and in addition to my supportive husband, I saw the smiling, approving face of Norman Brokaw, our agent. He had used his power and contacts to open up this important opportunity for me to prove myself as a solo act. I soon settled in and began feeling comfortable with my new surroundings. By the second week, I said to myself, *Hey, this stage is big, but it's all mine!*

When the *Solid Gold* opportunity came along, performing on my own gave me confidence to compete against a half-dozen other hopefuls— including Gladys Knight—for the cohost job. I was elated to be picked. The producers said I won because of my chemistry with Andy Gibb, who was the younger brother of Barry, Robin, and Maurice Gibb of the Bee Gees.

My *Solid Gold* duties included introducing the various acts and interviewing them on occasion, singing duets with Andy or other guest artists, and doing solo performances from time to time. Chatting onstage didn't come easy because when I was with the 5th Dimension, I just sang and smiled. When Billy and I did our duet thing, we split the talking, but he had to loosen me up, he said, because I sounded like a schoolteacher.

Billy: Marilyn didn't like it whenever I teased her by saying, "Hey, Teach."

Marilyn: I certainly felt like a schoolmarm compared to some of the acts we had on *Solid Gold*. One of the more extreme examples was Wendy O. Williams and the Plasmatics. Wendy had starred in some adult videos in the mid-1970s before moving from porn to punk as the front woman for a thrash metal band called the Plasmatics. She frosted the tips of her Mohawk haircut and sometimes wore nothing more than bits of electrical tape on stage. For *Solid Gold*, she wore something more substantial—a black breastplate mold with accentuated breasts and nipples, black leather pants with slits, and towering platform shoes.

During rehearsal, I noticed technicians setting a half-dozen inexpensive television sets on the stage in preparation for the Plasmatics' appearance.

"What are those TV sets for?" I asked a technician.

"They're part of the show," he replied. "Wendy's going to smash them."

I was shocked by the wanton destruction that would appear on national TV, but then things got creepy when I noticed that someone had drawn a pentagram—a symbol associated with Satanism—on the floor. I retreated to my dressing room and called Billy.

"Baby, you will not believe what's going on down here," I exclaimed. "The Plasmatics have a pentagram on the floor as part of the set design. This is about as satanic as you can get."

"You be careful," he said. "And you stay away from them."

"Don't worry. I'm going to pray before I go out there and be a light."

I had drawn the short straw to introduce the group. I prayed for the Lord's protection, and when I was done, I stepped back and watched Wendy walk on stage wearing contact lenses with slits straight up and down—to effect the look of cat eyes, I suppose. The Plasmatics dived into a heavy-metal cut called "Black Leather Monster" as the stage filled with smoke.

A studio audience of zombie-looking fans—several guys had spiky mohawks while others preferred the gothic look—went berserk. They danced wildly and flailed their arms, which struck others. Several fights broke out, prompting security to rush in and restore order on the set.

Most of the time, though, things were tamer on *Solid Gold*. Charlie Daniels, the country singer, was a sweetheart and a gentleman. We enjoyed helping new acts get their big break. An Australian band, Men at Work, thanked me profusely for having them on the show, although I had nothing to do with the booking.

Andy Gibb, who was always kind and a gentleman to me, departed after one season with *Solid Gold*. The year we spent together was difficult for Andy. He was involved in a very public love affair with Victoria Principal, and rumors of his drug problem were fueled by his tardiness and absences on the set. Whatever was going on, the love between him and his family was very evident. When Andy left, I missed them all.

I continued to host the show for four more years, which afforded me great visibility and gave my fledgling solo career a boost. We had some extraordinary talent as regulars on the show. I had great fun with puppeteer Waylon Flowers and his wild, wacky "Madame," until he became ill. He subsequently died of a frightening new disease called AIDS. The comic genius of Arsenio Hall caught everyone's attention, and I knew great things were in store for him.

I have always believed that *Solid Gold* was a blessing from the Lord because it felt very much like God put me there to be a witness to others. I received wonderful letters from those who would say, "I know you're a believer, and I can see the Lord in you." I also received critical letters that said things like, "You can't be a Christian and be on that show. Those dancers are so scantily clad, and the way they shake their bottoms . . ." My answer to them was that I was not the producer, I was not the director, and I didn't own the show. I was a paid employee like everyone else, and I couldn't stop the dancers from doing what they were doing or the way they were shot. All I had control over was how I was seen and what I said.

Billy: People told me that they could see the Lord in Marilyn when she was on *Solid Gold*. Sometimes she didn't look like she was part of the show when those wild and over-the-top acts were on.

Marilyn: Billy handled my *Solid Gold* success fine during the early 1980s. What he didn't handle well was his drinking. Even after he came back to the Lord, Billy continued to imbibe.

Billy's drinking had bothered me long before I scolded him for messing up my wedding, but I never viewed him as an alcoholic in those early years of marriage. *Alcoholic* was such an ugly word and frightening prospect. I knew Billy drank a lot, but he was a "happy drunk," a guy who held his liquor well and who knew how to have a good time. Besides, I was used to people drinking around me because I came from a family where alcohol played a significant part in our lives. Friends of my parents came over quite often to socialize and talk politics. When they allowed me to horn in from time to time with a song, they always had drinks in their hands.

I drank some, too, beginning with my years at UCLA. Billy always drank more than I did, but I didn't think it was a big deal until one time early in our marriage. Billy had some friends over to the house, including Sonny Porter. Billy drank quite a bit that evening, and then we got into an argument in front of his friends. He ordered me out of the room—and when I didn't comply fast enough, he kicked at me and brusquely pushed me down the hall toward the master bedroom.

The experience humiliated and frightened me, and I felt that he had crossed over a huge line in our marriage.

I had heard stories about drinking husbands who abused their wives. I had promised that I would never allow myself to be put into a situation like that. Now, this had happened. I retreated to my bedroom, crying and upset. I decided that that evening was not the right time to say anything because he was too volatile. The next day, however, I would wait until he left the house before I collected some things and left him. Then he would return to an empty house.

I woke up resolved to make good on my plan. I said nothing to Billy, but I wasn't my normal jovial self, and I'm sure that even he could see that our relationship was clearly strained. Billy must have realized something was amiss because he started apologizing for the way he behaved the previous evening—without any prompting from me.

"I'm sorry, Marilyn," he pleaded. "I don't know why I did what I did. I promise you that it will never happen again. Please forgive me."

I accepted his apology, but he could tell that I wasn't happy with the way things had gone. Since this was the first time he acted physically abusive toward me, I gave him a second chance, but in the back of my mind, I thought, *If this ever happens again, I'm out of here.*

Billy made good on his promise not to physically abuse me again, but he continued to drink his Seagrams VO, sometimes pouring his first glass before noon. I was convinced Billy had a serious drinking problem, which prompted me to read some material about alcoholism. The descriptions of an alcoholic fit Billy to a T.

One day I told Billy what I had learned. "Baby, do you realize that I think you are an alcoholic?" I asked.

Billy: I laughed because what she was saying sounded so preposterous. "Me? An alcoholic? You must be nuts."

Marilyn: "No, I'm not," I replied calmly. "I've been reading these articles, Baby, and they say if you drink every day, and always have to have alcohol whether you're with people or alone, then you're probably an alcoholic."

Billy: "But I've been doing these things for a long time, so I'm not an alcoholic," I said. That's what I believed. I liked a shot or two of Seagrams VO during the day to get me going. I liked to drink fine wine with dinner, and if someone presented me with a nice bottle of cognac after dinner, I didn't say no.

Marilyn: The fact is Billy could sip all day and not have it affect him. On some occasions, though, alcohol *did* affect him in ways that he couldn't see. One afternoon we were riding a New York subway with Florence and Marc. Billy, who had been nipping at his VO since lunchtime, was talking way too loud. "Hold your voice down," I scolded. "Everyone can hear what you're saying."

Billy: I didn't like her tone of voice. She was putting me down. "So I'm getting loud, huh?" I taunted.

She said, "Yeah, you're getting loud, and you're embarrassing me, so pipe down."

"You want to hear loud? Here's loud." I stood in the middle of the subway car and yelled at the top of my lungs. The people around me started moving away. I turned to Marilyn and said, "Now *that's* loud."

Marilyn: What a scene! Florence started giggling, which caused Marc to say, "Shut up," and then the whole thing deteriorated. I was so embarrassed that I slid down in my seat and wished I could disappear.

We clashed for many years over his drinking. Billy got so tired of denying he was an alcoholic that he decided to prove me wrong by not drinking for one year.

Billy: I stopped drinking on January 1, 1978, which meant that during the Christmas holidays and New Year's Eve, I knocked myself out. Celebrated like I always did. When I woke up on New Year's morning, though, that was it. I was quitting cold turkey.

Those first few days were shaky. I fought headaches and felt awful, but I laid off all through January and right into February and March. When June rolled around, I was still on the wagon, but I had a fortieth birthday coming up on June 26. We flew back to St. Louis for a big homecoming and reunion, and my parents threw a party for me. The Big Four-Oh was something to celebrate, right? I couldn't see how I could celebrate without having one teensy-weensy drink.

Marilyn: I tried to talk Billy out of taking that first drink because he still had another six months to go, but he was determined to have his "one" drink to celebrate his special birthday. Wouldn't you know it—he couldn't stop with one drink. Billy tumbled off the wagon with a resounding thud and went right back to his old habits.

Billy: I messed up, but I still wanted to show Marilyn that I could stop drinking for a year. A couple of years later, I started another alcohol fast on January 1. The same thing happened—I made it to my birthday again, but then it was too hard to stay away from my whisky and wine!

Marilyn: So Billy fell off the wagon again. After this second occurrence, Billy accepted that he couldn't stop drinking for a year, so he decided he would stop drinking the heavy stuff. No more Seagrams VO; hello wine, champagne, sherry, port, and beer. He also decided that cognac was a form of strong wine.

Billy: What I did to compensate for not having the heavy stuff was to drink more of the weak stuff, but that approach didn't work. Then I hid several bottles of cognac in the butler's pantry. I couldn't walk past that pantry without wanting a drink.

Marilyn: One night in 1986, we were invited to a party at Burt Reynolds' house. He lived within walking distance, a block from us. I had acted in a play at the Burt Reynolds Jupiter Theater in Jupiter, Florida, and gotten to know Burt a little bit. This was a serious Hollywood party. Carol Burnett was there, along with heavyweights like Ryan O'Neal, Christina Ferrari, Charles Durning, and Tom Selleck, to name a few. The champagne flowed like tap water.

Billy *drank* the champagne like it was water. Then Burt announced that he wanted to play a game called "Win, Lose, or Draw," which he was getting ready to introduce on television as a game show. Burt divided us into groups to play. Billy was a little snookered, so when the questions came his way, he offered up outlandishly wrong answers. People were turning around and giving me looks that I felt said, *That's your husband?*

I was totally embarrassed. The next day I told him how I felt. "You might not care how people look at you, but I care about how people look at me. And you reflect me!"

I think that had an impact on him, but he still hadn't gotten it. A few days after that, Billy drove down to San Diego on business and returned the same night totally drunk. I was so angry with him. "You could have killed somebody!" I yelled. "You could have killed yourself."

Billy: I don't know how the Rolls made it back—the angels must have taken the steering wheel. To make it home in my inebriated state was only by the grace of God. Driving drunk was not smart. That was the beginning of my realization that something had to give. It was time to take another look at who I was. Marilyn said that alcohol was taking a toll on my body and on our relationship. Deep down, I knew she was right.

I thought about the times I sat in church on a Sunday morning and heard Pastor Ingram say that if alcohol controlled your life, then you better cut it out. I felt convicted that I needed to do something, especially after barely remembering the trip home from San Diego. I finally admitted to myself and to my God that I had an illness. It was time to release it into the Lord's hands and get help.

I committed myself to Alcoholics Anonymous and gave the Lord my problem. That first AA meeting at a bank building in Beverly Hills was a lulu. I saw famous faces and met a lot of alcoholics and drug addicts. I didn't know how difficult it would be to stand up and say, "My name is Billy Davis, Jr., and I'm an alcoholic."

Relief flooded through me after I made my declaration. I had let it go. I had been drinking for forty years, but now I promised myself that I would go for another forty years without a drop.

I went through AA's 12-step program, and since I believed in a higher power, I took dead aim at this terrible disease. I admitted that I was powerless over alcohol and that my life had become unmanageable. I was ready to have God remove these defects in my character, and I humbly asked Him to remove this shortcoming in my life.

I have been dry for nearly twenty years, so I'm halfway there. If I had known I would feel this good, I would have stopped years ago!

Marilyn: I'm so proud that Billy no longer drinks, and his determination to make this major change in his life led to major improvements in our marriage. It had been impossible to rely on Billy to make important decisions when he wasn't alert enough half the time. I like the sober Billy much better. Now I have a greater respect for him in all areas—and performing with him became a lot more fun.

During this effort to get Billy to do something about this drinking, God was working in my life, too, because I had to grow as well.

"My life changed, too, after

I started reading the Bible.

I realized that the Lord

had been watching me

all through the years."

CHAPTER 12

A CHANGE IS GONNA COME

It's been a long, a long time coming, but I know . . .

Marilyn: I experienced tranquility when I came to the Lord, which I can only describe as a peace in my spirit. I prayed daily. I read my Bible daily. I thanked the Lord for my blessings: a roof over my head, my good health, the health of my loved ones and good friends, and peace in our country. The more I thanked Him, the more grateful I became for the things I had taken for granted.

My understanding of the Bible opened up like a rose petal—just like Bunny Wilson said it would if I prayed each time before I cracked open the pages of God's Word. I can remember reading a margin note in my *Spirit-Filled Life Bible* that said, "Faith unlocks our understanding of Scripture." I nodded because I was finding out that was *true*.

Scripture was showing me that the most important people from the world's point of view were merely people in God's view—no more, no less. Those who thought they were intellectually superior—and I included myself among those at one time—had a surprise coming because in

1 Corinthians 1:19, God said, "I will destroy the wisdom of the wise; the intelligence of the intelligent I will frustrate" (NIV).

The Lord was more interested in how I would serve Him, a principle that Jesus discussed in a parable called The Ten Talents. How was I using the talents that the Lord gave me? For God's glory or my gain?

For my gain would ultimately be futile since we can't take any Grammy awards or fat bank accounts with us when we die. I now saw my singing career in a different light. Now I was singing for a different audience—the Lord—which changed my whole focus for living. My career was no longer my be-all and end-all. Sure, that aspect of life was still important to me, but it stopped being my main focus. An interesting thing became obvious to me: When I stopped trying to control my career, things happened. When I tried to create opportunities for myself, things didn't happen.

My relationship with God became a love affair. I realized that God, who loved me so much, created me for His pleasure. Now I wanted to please Him. I could do that through my singing, and I could please Him by being a better wife to Billy. I started encouraging Billy more often. When he voiced his ideas, I didn't automatically put him down. Instead, I listened thoughtfully, and if there was something I could add to the discussion, I merely offered my thoughts for consideration.

Then the Lord showed me another thing I could do to improve myself—stop being such a perfectionist. Being perfect had been ingrained into me at a very young age. I wish I could blame the nuns at Mother Mary Mission Catholic School for rapping my knuckles whenever I made a mistake in cursive writing, but this streak ran in my family.

My stubborn struggle for perfection followed me into my adult life and impacted how I interacted with those who knew me well. Prior to coming to the Lord, I could be difficult to be around when it came to my music and my marriage to Billy. Regarding the former, *all* the notes had to be right. If Florence, Ronald, or Lamonte—or my lovely husband—sang off key in rehearsal, I made sure they knew it. If they missed a note in *concert*, I mentioned it in the dressing room afterward. The reason I made a big deal about every note being right is because I believed that even an untrained ear—which describes 99 percent of our audiences—could detect a discordant sound. I hated it when our music was sung wrong.

The attitude about being perfect extended to my interactions with Billy. I always "knew better" about anything and everything, and I even corrected Billy—in public—about the right way to pronounce words or cities we were traveling to. I had a problem when I felt he didn't measure up to the standard I thought a husband and life companion should be. I badgered him for years—poor baby!

The Lord began showing me that having a perfectionist spirit didn't make anyone happy to be in my presence. I was always comparing things to some imaginary level that I could never achieve. Reading the Bible showed me that I didn't need to prove myself to God. Since He had accepted me just as I am, why couldn't I extend the same grace to others? Besides, there was nothing I could do to improve myself in God's eyes.

Bunny Wilson gave me some great words of encouragement. She said that I didn't *have* to change anything about my life after I came to the Lord, but I would *want* to change as I learned more about God and His plan for my life.

As I began praying about my attitude, I listened to the Holy Spirit. He immediately showed me opportunities where I could cool it. For instance, I would participate in a conversation with Billy and several others, and the conversation would be flowing along, and then I would have a great thought that I just *had* to share with everybody. When that happened, I wanted to speak up so badly that I stopped listening to whoever else was talking and concentrated on when that person would take a breath—so I could interject my thoughts. What happened more often than not, however, was that my comment—the one I just *had* to share—usually wasn't constructive to the conversation at all. In more instances than not, my opinion had the wrong impact.

When this happened, I wished I could take back my intemperate comment, but words, once spoken, can't be retrieved. That's why I started praying about this aspect of my character, saying, "Lord, please help me to stop putting my foot in my mouth."

The most interesting thing happened. The Holy Spirit started giving me "checks" in my spirit. Suddenly, I could feel this thing inside my heart saying, *No, don't say that. Now's not the right time.* I think I had to bite my tongue the first few times I felt those checks, but I noticed that when I held back from declaring what I thought was so important, five minutes later I realized what I had to say wasn't that important.

Billy: Regarding Marilyn's perfectionism, I knew what Marilyn was reaching for—to do the absolute best in everything we did—but I also knew that perfection didn't exist. Even if we think something is perfect, someone else may not agree. Sometimes when you're pushing hard to get something, you put other people on the defensive. You anger them. When you keep pushing people hard, you want more and more, not realizing that someone is giving you all they can give.

People might have thought that Marilyn was being hard on me, correcting me, or trying to make me come off right in public. But that didn't bother me. I knew how she was. She didn't mean any harm; she just had a problem sometimes picking the right time to say something.

Marilyn: I could feel my perfectionistic skin being shed bit by bit every time I listened to the "check" in my spirit. Billy noticed it right away because this impacted our marriage. Instead of arguing about the fastest way to LAX, I let Billy drive the route he wanted to go. Funny, but we always made good time to the airport—and we both arrived less stressed. Instead of throwing out opinions right and left about how our careers should go, I listened to what Billy had to say. Our marriage improved immensely when this happened. The marital spats dwindled to a trickle.

Billy: Just as Marilyn could see how I changed after I stopped drinking, I could see a huge difference in Marilyn's attitude toward me when she started working on her perfectionism. Our relationship improved so much—it was like we were trying to see who could serve each other the most.

My life changed, too, after I started reading the Bible. I realized that the Lord had been watching me all through the years. Sometimes when I was driving along and thinking quiet thoughts, He showed me visions of my past:

Remember the time when you were standing on the steps and that gang member had a knife pointed at your stomach and said he was going to gut you?

I was there.

Remember the time you got shot?

I was there.

Remember the time you almost drowned in Hawaii?

I was there.

Remember the time when you took your family and a friend of Steven's on a weekend trip in a motor home high into the mountains in the middle of winter, and the motor home slid on black ice and you nearly tumbled off a cliff?

I was there.

It was great how the Lord let me see how He had been there every step of the way, including my decision to quit drinking and beat alcoholism. God laid other things on my heart, including a desire to become my "brother's keeper." I felt the Lord wanted me to be of service to others—to make a difference in people's lives by giving my time, my talents, and—yes—my money. Marilyn was totally on board with me.

I am reluctant to speak in any detail about what Marilyn and I have done to help others in need, since Jesus spoke out against that. In Matthew 6 (TLB), Jesus says, "Take care! Don't do your good deeds publicly, to be admired, for then you will lose the reward from your Father in heaven. When you give a gift to a beggar, don't shout about it as the hypocrites do—blowing trumpets in the synagogues and streets to call attention to their acts of charity! I tell you in all earnestness, they have received all their reward they will ever get."

These days Marilyn and I are excited about participating in service to the Lord. I think we got involved in the right way. For instance, we didn't jump into anything right after our "Jesus at the Roxy" experiences because we weren't anxious to get out there talking about the Lord until we knew what we were talking about. That meant going to Bible studies and listening to some good Bible teaching on Sunday mornings. We learned that you don't have to have the answer to every question. It's okay to say, "I don't know."

After a good year of reading God's Word, Frank Wilson asked us to accompany him to prisons, and that started our involvement with various prison ministries. We have performed at outreach events for the Billy

Graham and Luis Palau Evangelistic Associations. Marilyn used her *Solid Gold* experience to cohost the annual Children's Miracle Network Telethon and the United Negro College Fund Telethon, and I performed on these telethons as well. Marilyn also cohosted Christian events such as the "Dove Awards" (with Glen Campbell) and the "Stellar Gospel Awards" (with Clifton Davis). Together, we even did a "Jesus at the Roxy"–type event at the Shrine Auditorium with—you guessed it—Pastor Billy Ingram.

There was one thing the Lord laid on my heart that I didn't want to do, however. When He prompted me to start a "praise outreach" music ministry, I ignored Him. I didn't want to do it. But He kept placing it on my heart that this was my assignment from Him. It's an awesome thing to realize that God has a special plan for you and is pursuing you to fulfill it. I told Marilyn that the Lord was leading me to start a ministry called Soldiers for the Second Coming, and she understood that this was something I had to do. For more than five years, we've been holding these outreaches two to three times a month at various churches in Southern California.

On these evenings, we invite anyone to join us for some great singing and testimonies about how God is working in people's lives. Afterward, we serve food for the fellowship time, provided by the ministry. I love going to Costco and buying barbecued honey chicken drumsticks by the bushel and preparing the food for everyone to enjoy.

Marilyn: I used to think that the saying "It's more blessed to give than to receive" was kind of cornball until I started doing it God's way and found out that it is truly more blessed to give than to receive. Now I love when I can give of myself to make a difference in the lives of others, which often helps strengthen their faith.

My new attitude about life and perfectionism helped when talk resurfaced about the original five members of the 5th Dimension reuniting in the late 1980s. Our managers, Erik Sterling and Jason Winters, planted the seeds about a reunion. They had been managing the 5th Dimension (comprised of Florence, Ronald, Lamonte, and our replacements) for several years. Erik and Jason had become close friends, and Billy and I were so impressed with them—they were visionaries and totally committed to their artists—that we asked them to represent us. They felt that a reunion would be a great fit, so toward the end of 1990, we decided to reunite on stage with Florence, Ronald, and Lamonte.

George Bush (number forty-one) was the president of the United States back then, so it seems appropriate to say this was a "kinder, gentler" version of the 5th Dimension. What a difference twenty-five years made since we had formed in 1965. We were more mature in our ways and our actions. We were mellower and more giving. The five of us decided early on that we would not make one person more important than the other, and we would divide the money equally among the five members as we had in the past. We joked that none of us wanted to go back to our bickering United Nations days.

In rehearsals, I didn't huff and puff when someone hit a wrong note. Then I learned that we had to rescore some music because some of our music charts had been misplaced over the years. That was a costly undertaking, which cut into our profits, but I let it go by. Before I would have thrown a conniption and said, "What do you mean, you lost the charts?"

Billy: Our first reunion date was a weeklong engagement the last week of December 1990 at Trump's Plaza—a Donald Trump casino on the Atlantic City boardwalk. When we were introduced as the "original 5th Dimension," we were showered with a spontaneous standing ovation—such an overwhelming roar of applause that most of us were in tears. We did all the hits, plus some new material, and like the old days at Nero's Nook, we wrecked the place. The reviews were great.

We had a wonderful time singing with Florence, Ronald, and Lamonte again. It's very special when you can do this with those with whom you share a common history. We especially enjoyed those "remember when . . ." moments where it was fun to see if your memory was right or wrong. Marilyn and I now had three more people who could say, "No, that's not the way it happened. It happened this way." The 5th Dimension reconnected in a special way that time can never change.

After Atlantic City, our reunion took a six-month hiatus until the summer of 1991, when we performed at various venues around the country. Playing at the Greek Theater in Los Angeles that August felt like a homecoming. Our performance netted this review from Dennis Hunt of the *Los Angeles Times*: "Nostalgia shows can often be dated, dull, and embarrassing—particularly if the artists have no sense of humor about their oldies and have deteriorated physically and musically. When the 5th Dimension was reunited at the Greek Theater on Saturday after a fifteen-year split, the pop-soul vocal quintet re-created the rich, soaring harmonies of its late-Sixties heyday, and had the good sense to poke fun at itself and some of its oldies."

We continued to do concerts throughout the 1990s as the "Original 5th Dimension" whenever we could work it into our schedule. Some concerts were what we called "private corporate jobs," when we would be asked to perform at special events held by corporations, such as their annual conferences or award banquets. Our last date together was in 1997. Shortly after that, Ronald retired.

Meanwhile, Marilyn and I continued to sing as a duet, and together with Erik, Jason, and our musical director Gail Deadrick we came up with a show called "It Takes Two," which was a celebration of the rock and soul duets from the Sixties, Seventies, and Eighties. Many acts that we paid tribute to no longer performed together, like Marvin Gaye and Tammy Terrell, Sam and Dave, and Ike and Tina Turner.

Marilyn: We also stayed involved in various projects that came our way. In 1999, a producer named Jeffrey Finn approached us about doing a Duke Ellington tour in some of the smaller, secondary theaters around the country. That's what artists do when you're known for your singing ability but don't have any hits out. Duke Ellington was a composer, jazz musician, and band leader from the 1930s and 1940s who wrote many Broadway standards—"Take the A Train," "Sophisticated Lady," and "Hit Me with a Hot Note."

We went out on the road for three months and had a wonderful time performing a production built around Billy and me. Our conductor Jim Vukovich wrote complex jazz arrangements that incorporated four gifted singers and dancers, plus three musicians. Our friend and assistant Randy Jeffries did a superb job holding together a hectic schedule, which reminded us of our early years of one-nighters with the 5th Dimension. When the Duke Ellington tour was over, we resumed our "It Takes Two" dates in June 1999.

That's when I nagged Billy to get his annual physical—nagged because he'd gone without a thorough exam for nearly two years. I couldn't say that I blamed him for his reticence: I've heard that no male enjoys bending over for the infamous "prostate exam." That's when we discovered his prostate had an elevated PSA reading—18.

Dr. Holden, the urological surgeon with Cedars-Sinai, suggested doing a biopsy because of his high PSA number. "I promise you that this will be a breeze," Dr. Holden said. Billy wasn't convinced, but he understood the urgency of the situation: Without a biopsy, we would have no idea what we were up against, so he agreed to it.

Within two weeks, Dr. Holden performed the biopsy, taking cells and tissues from six different points in and around the prostate. Now it was a matter of waiting for the results to come back from the lab. Several days later, I was home when Billy took the phone call from Dr. Holden.

"Well, Billy, I need to let you know you have prostate cancer," the surgeon began, letting that thought sink in for a moment before plowing ahead. "We know it's there, and we need to do something about this," the surgeon declared.

Billy was stunned by the news. He listened quietly as Dr. Holden continued. "I know this news affects you and your wife, so maybe the both of you should come into my office so we can sit and talk about it."

The grave look on Billy's face told me he was scared. After relaying the conversation to me, he said to the doctor, "I better take care of this because it's not going away. We have to confront this sooner or later, so it would be better if we make it sooner."

When I heard that Billy had cancer, my thoughts turned morbid. People die from cancer. How long had cancer cells been swirling in Billy's body? How far had it spread? Did we catch it in time?

Dr. Holden said that we wouldn't have answers to those questions until we completed additional testing. What we could do in the meantime, he counseled, was educate ourselves about prostate cancer and the treatment options available to us.

Billy and I drove to the Beverly Hills library and learned a few things about cancer and the prostate. Cancer is the second leading cause of death in the United States—second only to heart disease—claiming more than 500,000 lives each year. Prostate cancer is the second most common cause of cancer death in men; lung cancer is number one.

Regarding treatment, Dr. Holden boiled it down to three options:

- removing the prostate—a prostatectomy

- submitting to radiation

- using seed implants

All three treatments were considered valid and good. Dr. Holden urged us to follow the surgical route, but Billy wasn't too excited to get "cut on," as he called it. No doubt that a prostatectomy was invasive surgery in probably the most sensitive part of the body for a male, and the chance of being rendered impotent was high—a shocking 59 percent chance, according to a study released by the *Journal of the American Medical Association*.

Radiation therapy had a downside. One of the things we learned was once you have radiation, you can't come back to the doctor and ask for a prostatectomy—there's nothing to remove since radiation burned up the gland. If you have the prostate removed by surgery, however, and cancer remains in the body, you can come back with radiation.

The third option, seed implants, did not appeal to us. My mother's brother, Uncle Harold, was stricken by prostate cancer, and he had chosen seed implants. That treatment didn't work for him, and he died.

We discussed these options with Dr. Holden. Yes, he admitted, a prostatectomy was invasive, and the risk of impotency was worth noting, but he said that in his practice, the percentage rate was much lower than the national average.

This was one of those times when Billy had to make the final decision totally without my comments. It was his body. If I influenced his thinking and it didn't work out, that was something I could never live with, even though my perfectionistic attitude loved giving my opinion on important matters. This time, I realized, the Lord was in charge. We prayed about it and asked the Lord to reveal to Billy or me what path we should take to save Billy's life.

Billy: I was seeing one of the top prostate cancer specialists, Dr. Patrick Walsh, and he was telling me that he was confident that the cancer was confined to the prostate, which was why he was also recommending a prostatectomy. Then Dr. Walsh received a phone call. "If you'll excuse me for a moment," he said.

I was left alone in the doctor's office, and I heard the Holy Spirit say to me, *Go ahead, have the surgery.*

"What, Lord?" I asked out loud. "I want to be sure I heard You right since You know that I don't want to be cut on."

Have the surgery, and you'll be all right.

When I saw Marilyn, I said, "Call Dr. Holden and set up the surgery."

Marilyn: That's what I did, and Dr. Holden set a date: August 27, 1999, at Cedars-Sinai Medical Center in Los Angeles.

Several weeks before the surgery, Billy and I were offered a recurring role on the TV sitcom "The Jamie Foxx Show," playing the parents of Jamie Foxx's girlfriend, played by a pretty actress named Garcelle Beauvais. I guess they needed a couple who knew how to argue, so we got the call. (Just a joke.) Learning our lines was a nice diversion from the reality that a prostatectomy was in Billy's future.

Billy and I both had a lot to worry about, but we knew that his life was in God's hands, and we were okay with that. Dr. Holden, his surgeon, told us that if he opened Billy up and discovered cancer *outside* the prostate, then he would not remove the prostate. Instead, Billy would have to go through radiation therapy later.

Billy: That was the first thing I groggily asked when I came out of surgery. "Did they take the prostate?" When the nurse said yes, I knew that was a good sign. My next question was, "Did they cut any nerves?" You see, while I wanted to live, I also wanted to *live*.

There were no complications, I was told. My doctors informed me that I should expect six weeks of recovery at the hospital and home, and nine months of healing time. Well, I healed up pretty good, and once I was back on my feet, I wanted to help out in the fight against prostate cancer, especially in the black community, where more black men die of prostate cancer than any other group. I told *Jet* magazine, "There's no reason for us to be dying like this. Some guys think checkups and prostate exams challenge their manhood. It's dangerous not to have exams, especially if you're black."

Marilyn and I participated in an educational video, "Not by Myself," and we appeared on the *Today Show*, where Katie Couric interviewed us about my prostate cancer experience and the importance of early detection through regular checkups.

Marilyn: Being involved in the fight against prostate cancer is just one of the things Billy and I are doing these days. We're still performing, although we find ourselves singing more in churches and at outreach events these days, which is fine by us.

People marvel that we've sustained a happy marriage for thirty-five years, especially in the entertainment world. How have we managed to do it?

The quick answer is that with God, anything is possible. We'll talk more about that in our next chapter.

"God's purposes for marriage are much higher and greater than our own."

CHAPTER 13

TOGETHER LET'S
FIND
LOVE

*I don't know much about this thing
called love, but I'm willing to try . . .*

Marilyn: Billy and I celebrated our thirty-fifth wedding anniversary upon the release of this book, and this milestone got us thinking. How many other marriages in Hollywood and the entertainment industry have lasted as long as ours?

Well, there's Paul Newman and Joanne Woodward, who married January 29, 1958, which means they'll be celebrating their golden anniversary in a few years. Actors Ossie Davis and Ruby Dee have been married longer—fifty-five years. Bill and Camille Cosby, who married in 1964, clung together even more when their only son, Ennis, was murdered in 1997. Sidney Poitier married actress Joanna Shimkus in 1976, so they are closing in on three decades. I'm sure we overlooked some couples, but today there aren't many celebrity marriages with more than twenty years on the odometer.

Let's face it—we live in an era when celebrity marriages can be measured in hour-long increments. Britney Spears was married for only fifty-five hours before seeking an annulment of her Las Vegas wedding. That's not a record, though. Hollywood celebrity Zsa Zsa Gabor was married for *one day*—the length of her 1982 marriage to Felipe de Alba. "I'm a marvelous housekeeper," said a defensive Zsa Zsa afterward. "Every time I leave a man, I keep his house!"

Despite their poor track record, Hollywood couples still want to tie the knot. Even the most jaded personalities seek the stability and companionship of a long-term relationship built on mutual trust and the desire to stay with each other "until death do us part"—unless they hedge their bets by publicly pledging to "stay with you for as long as I shall love you."

It isn't easy to stay married. Forget all the hit records and Grammy awards—Billy and I agree that our greatest accomplishment has been remaining married to each other for thirty-five years. Our marriage means so much to us that we didn't like it when people *thought* we had divorced.

This happened in the early 1980s during the height of my *Solid Gold* days. Cohosting the number one syndicated television program afforded me high visibility and media coverage. People were used to seeing Billy and me together, so when folks saw publicity shots or interviews of me without my husband, they leaped to a huge conclusion and assumed Billy and I had gotten a divorce.

Gossip, the Bible tells us in Proverbs 26:22 (TLB), "is a dainty morsel eaten with great relish." Well, Hollywood isn't that big a town, as the old saying goes, so it didn't take long for news of our "divorce" to make the rounds. It seemed like every time we ran into people we knew, we had to convince them that we were still married.

Billy: One time while Marilyn was working on *Solid Gold*, I traveled to a celebrity tennis tournament in New York City. A newspaper photographer snapped my picture, and the following day the caption underneath the photo identified me as the "ex-husband of singer Marilyn McCoo." The newspaper printed what they had heard. Then people at the tournament approached me and said, "Sorry to hear what happened. What are you going to do now?"

I became frustrated with the whole situation, and my attitude wasn't that good to begin with because I was battling vocal cord problems and didn't know whether I would ever sing again. I had to get this divorce business straightened out. When I got home, I asked our public relations firm, the Brokaw Company, to book us on talk shows so we could prove we were still together. Even after these public announcements, for years we ran into people all over the country who thought we had split up.

Marilyn: Going on these talk shows had an unintended benefit—we could talk about why we valued our marriage and placed so much importance on staying together.

God's purposes for marriage are much higher and greater than our own. In Genesis 2:18, God said it is not good for man to be alone, so He created Eve as the answer to the loneliness Adam was feeling. Even though Adam had a perfect relationship with God, a perfect environment, and had all the possessions he wanted, there was still a void of intimacy in Adam's life.

Our intimacy began long before we were physically intimate because Billy and I started with a friendship first. We *liked* each other long before we *loved* each other. I've known women who jumped into bed as soon as they were interested in a guy, but when that happened, their relationship tumbled because they weren't even friends yet. They overlooked unappealing aspects of their boyfriends' personalities because they wanted to keep the physical part going.

Billy: I'm the first to admit that Marilyn and I weren't wise enough to fully understand this principle in our early years, but I do know that as bad as our marriage got at times—the arguing, my drinking problems—a husband still has to take care of business. One time when we were in New York, Marilyn very much wanted to see *The Great White Hope*, a powerful play on Broadway starring James Earl Jones. Marilyn pulled some strings to scrounge up two tickets to this sold-out show.

On the afternoon of the evening performance, I met up with some buddies for some drinking. Marilyn says when I arrived back at the hotel room around four o'clock, I was smashed—really lit up. She was furious with me. "We have tickets to see the play tonight, and I'm going with you or without you!"

I apologized as best I could. "Don't worry, Baby, I'll be all right. Just let me take a little nap."

I lay down to sleep it off. When Marilyn woke me up two hours later, I got dressed and acted chipper because I didn't want to spoil her evening. You see, I had made a commitment to go to the play with her, and I didn't want to hurt my best friend, my wife. I wanted to make good on my promise to her, no matter what I had to do.

We arrived in time, and James Earl Jones's performance was as powerful as everyone said it would be. At the end of the first act, I turned to Marilyn and said, "Wow, Baby, I'm really glad we came to see this."

Marilyn: To his credit, Billy showed an interest in doing or seeing things I suggested. When we first got together, I introduced Billy to movies and plays he wouldn't ordinarily see, but I was careful with what I selected. I wouldn't take him to a play about women's struggles unless I read enough to know that men were enjoying it. I knew that foreign films requiring the reading of subtitles had to hold his interest from the opening credits. I discovered that Billy loved studying human behavior, so as long as there was movement in the story, he enjoyed accompanying me to those "artsy" films.

Efforts like this keep a marriage fresh, but I can remember a stale period when we went five years without taking an extended vacation. This was during the *Solid Gold* years when we were working separately. We enjoyed a long weekend from time to time, but we needed a longer stretch to reconnect and rekindle our romantic sizzle.

We cleared our schedules and treated ourselves to an extra-long trip—two and a half weeks in Europe and ten days in Morocco visiting my sister, Millie, who was stationed in the Foreign Service.

While we were abroad, we kept an open schedule, making daily plans as we arose. Leaving the responsibilities of home behind made our vacation so relaxing. I rediscovered Billy's wonderful sense of humor, one of the reasons I fell in love with him. The trip brought us closer again, and we promised ourselves we would not allow that much time to pass without reserving special time for the two of us.

Time together is essential for a healthy marriage. There is always something crowding our calendars, but we urge you to reserve at least one week a year for the two of you to get away by yourselves. Time away from the daily stress of work and children will help you remember what it was like when you fell in love with that special person you committed your life to. Getting together for a weeklong getaway will give you time to discuss your mutual goals and dreams for raising your children. Learning more about your spouse is a worthy pursuit.

One thing we've observed over time is that there are basic differences between men and women. Men don't change, as a rule. Billy was hanging his towel on the bathroom doorknob when we got married, and it's still there. Seriously, you can sand the edges off some of the corners, but what you see is what you get, for the most part. Women marry expecting men to change. Men marry expecting women not to change, but marriage rarely works that way.

I've talked to many women who've said, "I can't stand how my husband watches TV. We can never watch a program for longer than three minutes before he changes the channel."

"Was he like that before you got married?" I ask.

"Well, yes," she says. "I thought I could change him."

Surprise! That didn't happen.

What men need to know is that younger brides often go from being someone's daughter to someone's wife, which is a major adjustment for a woman who hasn't led an independent life prior to walking down the aisle. If she *has* been independent with a career, there are still many changes she will go through in her marriage. A woman's outlook will be different in her forties from the one she had in her twenties. I have met a number of women who, in their twenties, were so devoted to careers that the question of children never entered their minds. But as they approached their forties and became aware of their biological clocks ticking, they have made abrupt changes in their lives by wanting to have children and even showing a willingness to give up the careers that meant so much to them early on.

I have met women who have reached the pinnacle of success in their careers and lost their husbands in the process. They have then looked back on the loss and wondered if it was all worth it. So women, I advise you to seriously consider the mistakes that our sisters have made before us.

Spouses have a way of assuming they are always right and the other spouse is always wrong, so it was a good lesson for me to learn that I wasn't always right and Billy wasn't always wrong. When Billy's drinking problem was at its worst, I had an inflated attitude of my position in the marriage. I figured he wasn't in the loop because the booze incapacitated him. Billy didn't share that perspective, which caused conflict. Our marital issues reached such a low point in the mid-1970s that we sought a marriage counselor for several sessions.

With a third party in the room, I wasted no time describing all the things that Billy did wrong in our marriage. When I finished venting, the marriage counselor asked me to listen to what Billy had to say. My husband listed several qualities about me that bugged him, which was an eye-opener. I had really thought I had it together.

Billy: My nature is pretty laid back, but that doesn't mean I don't have opinions. At times, I felt that Marilyn wasn't listening to me because she thought I had been drinking or had nothing to say. When she listened to me, everything went fine. "I want to see more of that from her," I said to the counselor.

The counselor's insights helped us to see that we had been trying to change each other instead of accepting those qualities that had attracted us to one another in the first place. We had been trying to make each other into the person we thought we should be married to. Our marriage took on another tone when we stopped doing that.

Marilyn: Our counseling experience was such a positive thing that we recommend counseling for every couple *before* they get married. We have seen too many divorces resulting from not having serious discussions about serious matters prior to the wedding day. For instance, one person may want children, while the other would prefer to remain childless. Before they got married, though, they didn't talk about children because it always led to an argument. Couples may hope they can resolve issues like this when they're husband and wife, but that doesn't always happen.

Other touchy issues can be addressed in a premarital counseling situation. What happens if the prospective wife desires to stop working when children arrive but the husband-to-be has dreams of a lifestyle requiring two paychecks? Or, she may have set her sights on becoming a partner at the law firm, while he has visions of an Ozzie-and-Harriet family. Having a third-party counselor probe these important issues will help them work through these differences before the marriage.

Billy and I wish we had gone through premarital counseling, but it wasn't on our radar screens. I'm glad we did the next best thing, though, and sat down with a counselor when our marriage was taking on water. There's no shame in visiting with a third party. A good counselor can help each couple get the issues on the table.

Billy: There were times when I didn't have the patience to listen to Marilyn because she seemed to say the same things over and over again. When she sounded like a broken record, I just turned her off. When she accused me of shutting down, she was right.

One day I decided to listen to her even if it killed me. She made a lot of sense. Staying focused on what she was saying helped me learn about how she thought, how she developed ideas in her mind, and how she viewed life. I had missed the constructive things she sought to communicate to me.

My listening allowed me to tap into her thoughts, which I used for our benefit. I realized Marilyn had something to say that was important to our relationship and our growth as a couple. If we don't do that for each other, we're missing out on the best part of the relationship, which is communication from the heart. Now I look forward to what she has to say.

Marilyn: Speaking of communication, I always felt that Billy's grammar was not his strong suit. Growing up, I was always encouraged to use correct English. That's probably the reason Billy teased me about sounding like a schoolteacher. Because my husband would often struggle for words—or use the wrong words—when trying to communicate, I would discount what he said. I was so focused on his grammar that I missed the meaning of his message.

Sometimes I was embarrassed around other people, but others didn't have a problem understanding him. A wonderful influence in my life, actress Frances Williams, straightened me out one day. She told me that just because my thoughts came more quickly to me or that I expressed them more clearly didn't make them better. She said that Billy might take more time getting his ideas together, but when he spoke, they often revealed a deeper and more profound analysis. What a lesson I learned that day! I began to realize that as his wife, I should be encouraging him to express his thoughts, instead of finding fault with his syntax.

Billy: Even if you've had a better scholastic education than your spouse, that doesn't mean you're smarter. We've known people who had the best education money can buy, but they have trouble surviving in the world. You need to listen to each other. You need to find out those areas of strength in your spouse and use them to your advantage in your marriage.

Everyone has areas of strength, and everyone has areas of weakness. Regarding the latter, we know from talking to many couples that the area of finances can be deadly. Marriages come apart because of money. We've had our own differences.

Marilyn: For example, Billy has always had a gambling spirit when it comes to business, but we've lost money on many of his ventures.

I don't like to gamble, and I hate losing money. I feel that the career I chose was a major gamble in itself, so I didn't require the additional thrill of whether one of Billy's business ventures or music acts hit the jackpot. Yet I had to respect my spouse's dreams and try to support him, while simultaneously defining a limit to which I was willing to go.

Billy: When I initially got involved in my various business efforts, I did so with the idea that one day, when there were no more hit records, we would have a successful flow of income to maintain our lifestyle. I had always admired my father's and grandfather's independent business spirit and wanted to follow in their footsteps.

Over time, however, I realized that my plans weren't working out like I had hoped. This was putting a strain on our relationship. If I continued to pursue these money-losing ventures, I would hurt Marilyn's and my future, and I didn't want to do that. The things I wanted to accomplish in business would require me having more resources—money—than were available to me. They would also require more time for me to acquire the knowledge that I needed. When I understood those things, I realized I was an entertainer first and needed to focus my energies more on that, which had always been my first love.

I have seen a lot of men travel this road. Our ambitions exceed our abilities; that's how we get hung up in it. I want to urge men to stick to what they know, and if they are going into something new, do as much research as possible so they will know what the pitfalls are.

Marilyn: Throughout this book, you've read how we argued and fought with each other. We argued because we wanted to change each other's mind because we were convinced that our position was the correct one. That attitude was so stupid that sometimes we had to laugh.

In order for the marriage of two headstrong people to survive, we had to learn how to communicate in a constructive way—fight fair. One of my early lessons, which probably came from my wise parents, was when you had a problem, you attack the action, not the person. For instance, you could state, "What a stupid thing to say," rather than, "You're stupid!"

After a lifetime in show business, I've developed a thick skin, so I can handle criticism of something I've done. But when Billy called me stupid, we went to war. We clashed frequently until he found a new way to express his displeasure.

If you can offer a suggestion for making something better, you can soften the blow:

Maybe if you try doing it this way . . .

or

Maybe this is a better way to make your point . . .

Crossing your arms and declaring, "That's not going to work" usually means that you'll get asked to come up with something better.

We had numerous explosions over comments that should have been said at another time. We didn't know that timing was everything. We thought back to how we liked to be talked to when we come offstage. When Billy and I—or any performer—finish a show, it's our most vulnerable time. We have put our total being on the line with the hope of giving the audience an enjoyable evening. All we really want to hear is "Great show!" We don't want to hear about a weak song or poorly sung notes.

Criticism is better received the next day. We do want to know how to improve our shows, but not while the applause is still ringing in our ears. Billy and I went through many ugly moments before we realized this. Using that wisdom, if your wife has prepared a special meal for the family, don't tell her at the dinner table that her dish doesn't taste good.

Billy: She might take your head off.

Marilyn: If your husband spent the afternoon toiling in the back-yard, don't tell him he did a bad job trimming the bushes. Wait a day or two.

Billy: It's never wise to say things to hurt your spouse in the heat of argument. Even when you're hopping mad, choose your words wisely. You can't take back words once they're spoken. Statements like this destroy the foundation of any marriage:

- I wish you were dead.

- You never satisfied me.

- I never loved you.

- You're nothing but a loser.

- I wish you'd never been born.

Don't use your spouse's weaknesses or take insecurities you've shared with each other in intimate moments and throw them in your spouse's face. You may have the last word, but the damage you inflict on your relationship will be hard to repair. The Bible says the tongue "is an unruly evil, full of deadly poison" (James 3:8 NKJV), but "a word fitly spoken is like apples of gold in settings of silver" (Proverbs 25:11 NKJV).

Marilyn: We thank God that our love for each other was strong during the rockiest moments of our marriage, which prompts us to describe what happened when Billy's son, Steven, came to live with us in the early 1970s.

This really was a *Fresh Prince of Bel Air* situation. Steven was moving from one world into another—from a predominantly black inner-city environment in Detroit into a predominantly white upper-middle-class community in the San Fernando Valley. To add to the pressures, his father and stepmother were known all over the country. The big difference was this was no television sitcom; this was real life.

We were not the picture-perfect family of that TV series with a stable home environment and a ready solution for every problem. Steven was not a quick-with-the-answers seventeen-year-old like Will Smith. He was a nine-year-old child used to responding to things he didn't understand with anger and silence. We hoped to give him the benefit of his father's influence at this crucial point in his life and to offer him opportunities that hadn't been available to him in Detroit. I felt I could have a positive impact on his life, encouraging him to try new experiences and express what was on his mind.

The big problem was that we didn't have the Lord in our lives or have great parenting skills. Billy and Edna had split up when Steven was just a year old, and Billy had lived in Los Angeles pretty much since then. I had no other children, and as a child, I hadn't helped raise any younger brothers or sisters.

Before he moved in, Steven spent his summers with us, but since we were part-time parents, Billy was more like a "Disneyland dad." Living year-round with us proved to be a totally different experience. With our numerous road trips, our time for bonding with him was limited, and I'm sure he felt uprooted each time we left town. It was like taking two steps forward and five steps back.

Phone calls weren't enough to address Steven's needs. Like any child, he needed face-to-face interaction. Our situation required a special and caring person to be there for him when we were away, but also someone who would stand up to him and tell him no when necessary. We found that person in Lilian Hawkins. A widow with no children, she grew to love Steven as her own; they became very close.

Steven was having adjustment problems—issues with kids at school and a rebellious attitude toward his teachers. While he loved his dad and me and wanted to please, no amount of conversation or punishments seemed to change his behavior. It all came to a head one day when we received a phone call from Lilian, telling us that Steven had gotten fired from his cafeteria job at school. The principal wanted to discuss the incident with us. We were shocked because this job had meant so much to him. You see, Steven had a habit of biting his nails. The person in charge of the cafeteria told him that because of sanitary requirements, he would have to stop biting them before he could work there.

This job was something he had sought out. We had been encouraging him to stop biting his nails for some time, and we hoped that this would inspire him to succeed. We should have recognized that this was a sign of the kind of stress he was feeling, but we learned that much later. We were proud when he presented us with his newly grown nails. He got the job.

When Lilian's call came, we had been gone from home less than three days. Billy talked to Steven and told him that we all must meet with the principal upon our return. Steven was embarrassed, frustrated, and probably devastated by the firing. This job was something he had truly wanted, and now, because of bad behavior, he'd lost it.

I was disappointed and baffled. If this was what he did to something he seemed to care so much about, was there any way to reach him? Did Steven need more help than we could give him? Had we made matters worse by bringing him to California and not giving him the support he needed?

When Steven had lived with us for three years, I felt like we were in over our heads. I wanted Steven to go back to his mother, but I felt guilty for thinking that way. I knew he needed his father, needed us, but we weren't home enough. I had to tell Billy how I felt. When I did, I burst into tears, but Billy's gentle, reassuring words put me at ease. He said this was something we would resolve together.

Billy didn't call me selfish or add to my guilt. His response removed my sense of feeling trapped in a situation with no way out, and I no longer wanted to send him away. I began to feel that maybe we could look for other solutions to Steven's problems. We could research new ways of getting him to communicate and share his feelings by seeking professional advice. With a fresh look at the overall situation and a renewed commitment to our family, my love for Steven grew and my relationship with him improved.

Steven stayed with us for three more years, and we would have preferred that he stay longer, but he was the one who decided to move back to Detroit to live with his mother. Today, we are a strong family.

The way Billy handled the situation with Steven showed me how selfless he could be in our marriage. He really came through in 1995 when I was offered the chance to act and sing in a restaged Broadway production of *Showboat*, considered one of the classics. Our longtime musical arranger and conductor Gail Deadrick, who had been with us since the beginning of our duet career, helped prepare me musically for this role of a lifetime on Broadway. *Showboat* was a musical treasure that beautifully painted a portrait of the ugliness of racism, marital discord, and abandonment. I was offered the opportunity to play the major role of Julie, made famous by Helen Morgan on Broadway and Ava Gardner in the film version.

Being part of a major Broadway production, with eight performances a week, meant that I had to live . . . near Broadway. I was concerned how Billy would respond because a fourteen-month move to New York City (and later Chicago to continue the run) required uprooting us. To my amazement, and for which I have been eternally grateful, Billy was very supportive of this opportunity for me, knowing that this was the fulfillment of one of my life's dreams.

"I can work just as easily out of New York or Chicago," Billy said, whose calendar was filled with engagements on cruise ships in those days.

Billy and our assistant, Randy Jeffries, packed up a Ryder truck with everything we'd need for a year and took a week driving across the country while I was rehearsing. That was an amazing sacrifice he made for me, which strengthened our relationship. You hear continually about wives traveling to different locations for their husbands' work, but Billy's willingness to move for me was such a wonderful thing.

Billy: I don't think what I did was that special. Marilyn would have done the same for me. What I'm looking forward to is our golden anniversary, if the Lord grants us the years. I'm not sure how we'll celebrate it, but there's a precedent. For our twenty-fifth wedding anniversary in 1994, Marilyn and I renewed our wedding vows before two hundred friends and family at a nice Century City hotel. Our good friend Frank Wilson officiated.

I can't wait to renew those vows again!

"We feel an incredible gratitude that our singing and our stories can impact people way beyond a simple concert."

CHAPTER 14

AQUARIUS/LET THE SUN SHINE IN

*Just open up your heart and
let it shine on in . . .*

Billy: One wet summer day in the early 1970s, the 5th Dimension
arrived at the New York State Fair in Syracuse, New York, for an afternoon performance. It was overcast and raining like crazy, delaying the
start of the concert, but people patiently sat in the grandstands waiting
for us to come on stage. The postponement was prudent because rain and
microphones can be a dangerous combination.

When the thunderstorms stopped, we moved ahead and started the
show. Our final number in those days was, as you would expect,
"Aquarius/Let the Sun Shine In," which always got people on their feet and
finished the concert with high energy. The weather was still dark and
gloomy, but at the *exact* moment when "Aquarius" switched to us singing
Let the sun shiiine in, the sun burst through the black clouds and lit up the
stage, covering the 5th Dimension and myself in bright sunlight. The over-
flow crowd couldn't help but notice this heavenly event, and they started
screaming and cheering, no doubt excited by the way the brilliant sunshine
illuminated us while we sang *Open up your hearts and let the sun shiiine in.*

When the sun broke through those black clouds, we almost stopped singing—it was one of the most amazing and unexplainable experiences that I had ever been a part of. We saw the audience point at the bright sun while it aimed a spotlight right to the center of our stage. We weren't Christians then, but what happened did feel very spiritual.

Marilyn: Incidents like that confirmed in our minds that "Aquarius/Let the Sun Shine In" was a special song, and it's one that Billy and I still enjoy singing thirty-five years later. We are still fascinated how a four-minute, forty-five second recording fusing two songs from a rock musical became an icon symbolizing the hippie generation of the late Sixties. If a filmmaker or documentary director wants to evoke the late Sixties period of American history, all he has to do is splice together some shots of hippies running around in a "love-in" with "Aquarius" playing in the background, and the mood has been set. The makers of the Tom Hanks film *Forrest Gump* used "Aquarius/Let the Sun Shine In" to symbolize the country's mood in the summer of '69. In another Tom Hanks movie, *Apollo 13*, the lunar module was named *Aquarius* by the National Aeronautics and Space Administration (NASA) before the ill-fated trip to the moon in April 1970.

Billy: For those of you too young to remember 1969, you have to trust us when we say the lyrics to "Aquarius" spoke to the times we were living in:

> *When the moon is in the seventh house*
> *And Jupiter aligns with Mars*
> *Then peace will guide the planets*
> *And love will steer the stars*

This is the dawning of the age of Aquarius
Age of Aquarius
Aquarius, Aquarius
Harmony and understanding
Sympathy and trust abounding
No more falsehoods or derisions,
Golden living dreams of visions
Mystic crystal revelations, and the mind's true liberations
Aquarius, Aquarius

Were Marilyn and I aware that the lyrics to "Aquarius" promoted astrology? Yes, and we plead guilty as charged. When we recorded "Aquarius/Let the Sun Shine In," we were into astrology. We weren't the type of folks who couldn't leave the house without reading our daily horoscope, but we paid attention to what the stars allegedly "foretold" about our lives. Astrology had widespread acceptance in the late Sixties, which explains why we had our signs inscribed on our wedding bands.

We have in our boxes of memorabilia a "5th Dimension Age of Aquarius Love Wheel" that you spin around and find out who's compatible to be your life mate. For instance, since my sign is Cancer, I should have married a Capricorn. And Marilyn, a Libra, should have married an Aries, which shows you how much the people who promote astrology know.

Marilyn: We were also into things like tarot cards in those days. Back in the late 1970s, when things slowed down for Billy and me, my sister Glenda told me about a friend who read tarot cards. "I'd like you to meet Elena," she said. "After she reads your tarot cards, you'll be amazed. She really calls it."

This conversation happened during my "searching" period, so I was up for a session with Elena. I found her businesslike and matter-of-fact as she studiously turned over cards while making pronouncements about me and my life. One thing that I recall her saying was that I would someday have a successful TV show. She said that she didn't know if I would be the star of the show or not, but I would be an integral part of the show's success.

"I need to tell you that pink is the color of success," she continued.

"What do you mean?" I asked. I wondered if I would have to dress in pink the rest of my life.

"You should always have pink flowers in the home and burn a pink candle and pink incense for success," Elena replied. "When you do this, I want you to sit quietly and concentrate on the candle burning and give thanks to the spirit that gave me the power to read your tarot cards."

Sounded good to me. She was a spiritual leader, right? I drove home, stopping along the way to purchase a pink rose, a pink candle, and pink incense. I set the flower into water, lit a candle and a stick of incense, and curled up in a rocking chair, giving thanks to her spirit for giving her the ability to read my tarot cards. I made sure Billy wasn't around because he would have thought I flipped out, which would have started a new argument.

I really did this. I think I went through this rigmarole two or three times before I said to myself, "This is ridiculous," and blew out the candle and the incense.

It wasn't long after that that we received the invitation from Frank and Bunny Wilson that started me down the road to accepting Christ, so whenever I tell this story, I say, "God looked at what was happening down here on Earth, and He said, 'That's it. Time to bring her in!' "

God may be saying it's time to bring you in. Have you thought about that? Have you pondered why you're reading this book?

I don't think God ever wastes anything when it comes to the lives He's given us. In my situation, I have lived enough years to realize how God had a hand in *everything* that has happened to me. He imbued within me a deep desire to sing ever since I was a young girl. During my formative years, I received rigorous vocal training and invaluable singing experiences that gave me the confidence to stand on a stage and sing my heart out.

Then Lamonte McLemore suggested that the five us do a little group singing. We had no idea where his idea was going, but the 5th Dimension experienced fabulous success in the first eighteen months of our formation, which is really "overnight" in our industry. Most artists labor for years before they get their big break—if it ever comes at all. I can't even imagine how many thousands and thousands of acts never witness the doors of opportunity swing open as they did for us.

When Billy and I left the 5th Dimension, we had a hit record and a Grammy award in our hands within a year of starting our duet venture. Five years later, I never sought out the cohost role with *Solid Gold*—the producers approached me. Since then, I have received many more blessings, including the release of my contemporary gospel album *The Me Nobody Knows* in 1991, which was nominated for another Grammy, and acting on Broadway in the production of *Showboat* from 1995–96.

After hoofing it on Broadway, singing in the White House, and performing before millions on the *Ed Sullivan Show*, you might think that singing in a small church in Poughkeepsie, New York, with several hundred in the pews would feel like a comedown to Billy and me.

Not at all. No matter how big or small our audiences are these days, we feel very fulfilled because every appearance and every performance gives us a wonderful opportunity to share our lives. We feel an incredible gratitude that our singing and our stories can impact people way beyond a simple concert. To Billy and me, that's awesome.

Billy: You know, everybody thinks the answer to happiness is fame and fortune. We encounter plenty of young people today, and when we ask them what they want to be, their eyes light up and they say, "I want to be a star!"

They don't say, "I want to be a singer," or "I want to be an actor," or a writer, or a producer. They say they want to be a star. So we ask them, "What does that mean to you?"

"Oh, that means we get to ride in limousines, we get to have our pictures taken, we get to make a lot of money, and we get to wear the baddest clothes." But when we start asking them how they see themselves accomplishing that, we receive blank stares. They have no idea.

Marilyn and I speak from experience when we say that all the glitz and the glamour, all the fame and the notoriety, and all the trappings of success will leave you empty until you fill that void with Jesus Christ. He has a wonderful purpose for your life, just as He had a wonderful purpose for the lives He gave us.

It's interesting. These days, not that many people have seen the musical *Hair*, but a lot of people have heard of the 5th Dimension's version of "Aquarius/Let the Sun Shine In" from the show. I've often wondered why God had Marilyn and me sing that No. 1 hit, but perhaps it's because the song's popularity continues to draw people to come see us perform today. When we sing "Aquarius" in churches or outreach events, we tell audiences that "Aquarius" may be a song about hope and the "dawning of the Age of Aquarius," but Jupiter aligning with Mars doesn't give anywhere near the hope that Jesus Christ can.

Only the bright light of Jesus Christ will burn for eternity, and that's whom Marilyn and I have put our trust in.

We pray that you will too.

CHAPTER 15

EPILOGUE

We couldn't end this book without letting you know what happened to the original members of the 5th Dimension:

- **Florence LaRue:** We see Florence and we attend the same church—Church on the Way, founded by Pastor Jack Hayford. Florence sings in the Gospel Choir when she's not traveling. She and Lamonte continue to perform as the 5th Dimension, along with three other members, headlining in Las Vegas, performing with symphonies in concert, and appearing at major venues around the world.

- **Ronald "Sweets" Townson:** Ronald died from complications of diabetes in 2001 at his Las Vegas home. He is survived by Bobette, his wife of forty-four years, and a son, Kyle. His oldest son, Kim, died of a heart attack in his forties. Their longtime marriage served as a great inspiration to the two of us. Without our "Sweet Man" (we called him that because of his love for all things sweet), the original 5th Dimension sound lives only in recordings and memories.

• **Lamonte McLemore:** Lamonte keeps himself busy singing with Florence on 5th Dimension dates, photographing beauties for *Jet* magazine, and still telling his wonderful, crazy jokes. Lamonte, who was single for many years, is happily married to Mieko. They make their home in Las Vegas. We share a special bond with Lamonte; he and Billy grew up together in St. Louis, and besides, he introduced us.

We are proud of the existence of *The 5th Dimension: Up, Up and Away/The Definitive Collection*. It's a two-CD set of all of our single releases, plus a few extras, that allows us to relive that special time in our lives. We are so thankful to have this as a legacy.

ACKNOWLEDGMENTS

First, we would like to lovingly acknowledge Florence LaRue, Lamonte McLemore, and Ronald "Sweets" Townson. Without you, our lives would have been much different.

Now we would like to thank the following people for making *Up, Up and Away* possible:

• Erik Sterling and Jason Winters, through their loving and watchful eyes, showed us that we had a story to tell that would bless people. They have guided us throughout this project. Our relationship, which is grounded in a long friendship, has grown and expanded in wondrous directions.

• Steve Rosenblum, Konrad Leh, Jon Carrasco, Stephen Roseberry, Andre Carthen, and Miles Robinson of Sterling/Winters showed us their love by always going far beyond the expected in everything they do for us.

• The Sterling/Winters team expended the energy to make this book happen and gave their enthusiastic and wholehearted support over the years.

- Mark Christensen moved our book project along at a crucial point and lifted us with his encouraging words.

- Our coauthor, Mike Yorkey, exhibited his vision, his discipline, and his commitment to expressing our voices.

- Greg Thornton, vice president of Moody Publishers, exhibited great enthusiasm and belief in this project, along with his patience in bringing it to completion.

- Our literary agent, Chip MacGregor with Alive Communications, worked diligently on this project and came through for us at a critical time.

- Frank and Bunny Wilson gave us their assistance in making this book happen and have provided us with spiritual guidance over the years.

- Joel Strote displayed his brilliant legal mind and "watched our backs" from the beginning to the end.

- Jonathan Exley generously contributed his amazing photographic gift in capturing the essence of our relationship in the cover photo.

- Laythan Armor and Scott Smith gave us their musical productions, which are included as a gift to you.

- Paul and Dianne Saber opened their beautiful home for a round of interviews and provided some wonderful insights into the manuscript.

- Amber Rogers and Nicole Yorkey transcribed our interviews and provided editorial support.

- David and Sandy Brokaw offered their help with this book at every turn and continue to be an important part of our lives.

- Jonathan Singer helped us to get the book started.

- Mel Berger was there in the beginning.

A special acknowledgment to Sonny Porter, Gail Deadrick, and Randy Jeffries for their years of commitment to us. You have many gray hairs in your heads with our names on them!

We thank God for the blessing of parents who knew the importance of a close family, and for our brothers and sisters who love us and continue to support us on our life's journey. Our son, Steven, is a major blessing in our lives, and it has been a joy watching him develop into the man he is today. You make us proud.

For their spiritual guidance and moral support, we acknowledge: Pastor Bob Rieth, Pastor Archie Dennis, Pastor Jack and Anna Hayford, Pastor Scott and Rebecca Bauer, Pastor Billy Ingram, Terri McFaddin, Dr. Barbara Williams Skinner, Bishop Charles and Mae Lake, Pastor John and Diana Cherry, Pastor John Barta, Pastor Cliff and Audree Ashe, Susan Stafford, Gigi Gamble, Derek and Nancy Lewis, Susan Munao, Soldiers for the Second Coming, Michael Lewis, and Darrell Alston.

We owe a debt of gratitude to people who were there at the beginning of our careers and have contributed so much: Johnny Rivers, Bones Howe, Jimmy Webb, Marc Gordon, Al Bennett, René DeKnight, Bob Alcivar, Norman Brokaw, Sam and Mary Haskell, Chris Burke, Ben Bernstein, Sara Boyers, Al Masini, Bob Banner, Lou Horvitz, Brad Lachman, Donald "Duck" McLemore, Jerry Rubenstein, Gil Segel, Otis Smith, Patti Dennis, Macey Lippman, Helene Taber, Larry Uttal, Irv Biegel, Don Davis, Eddie Beal, Marcellina Hawthorne, and Nate Neblett.

Our thanks to special friends who have stood beside us through the years: Manny and Willette Klausner, John Dunning, Claudette Dennis, Larry and Sandy Frankel, Calvin Bell, Millie Cook, Harry Elston, Carol Connors, Brenda Porter, Andi and Mike Jablow, Barbara Williamson, Bill Cosby, Robert and Donna Guillaume, Pat Boone, Kathy Ireland and Greg Olsen, Rudy and Susan Saltzer, Bob and Beverly Cohen, Irv and Marge

Cowan, Stan Schneider, Bev Scott, Fred and Susie Wehba, John Hamilton, Browning and K-lynn Yelvington, Tina Chatman, Kattie McCune, and Calvin Scott.

Thank you to our special fans who have loved us and supported us throughout our careers. You were the air that lifted our balloon to heights that we would have never imagined. We love you.

CONTACT INFORMATION

Marilyn McCoo and Billy Davis, Jr. are available for performances, speaking engagements, and media appearances. These days, they are invited to perform in concert at civic functions, church programs, charity events, prayer breakfasts, and other outreach events.

For more information about bringing Marilyn and Billy to your hometown, contact:

Konrad Leh
Sterling/Winters, Inc.
10877 Wilshire Blvd. #1550
Los Angeles, CA 90024
(310) 557-2700 phone
e-mail: Jwinters@sterlingwinters.com

You can also find them on the World Wide Web at:
www.marilynmccooandbillydavisjr.com

RECORDINGS

BILLBOARD'S TOP 40 HIT LIST
FOR THE 5TH DIMENSION

Date	Highest Position	Weeks On Top 40	Song Title	Label
2/4/67	16	7	Go Where You Wanna Go	Soul City
6/17/67	7	10	Up Up & Away****†	Soul City
12/9/67	34	1	Paper Cup	Soul City
2/24/68	29	5	Carpet Man	Soul City
6/22/68	3	12	Stoned Soul Picnic†	Soul City
10/26/68	13	6	Sweet Blindness	Soul City
1/11/69	25	6	California Soul	Soul City
3/15/69	1 (6 wks)	16	Aquarius/Let The Sunshine In**† (Billy Davis, Jr., lead vocal)	Soul City
8/9/69	20	7	Workin' On A Groovy Thing	Soul City

BILLBOARD'S TOP 40 HIT LIST
FOR THE 5TH DIMENSION (CONT'D)

DATE	HIGHEST POSITION	WEEKS ON TOP 40	SONG TITLE	LABEL
10/4/69	1 (3 wks)	14	Wedding Bell Blues† (Marilyn McCoo, lead vocal)	Soul City
1/24/70	21	6	Blowing Away	Soul City
5/2/70	24	5	Puppet Man	Bell
6/27/70	27	5	Save The Country	Bell
11/21/70	2 (2 wks)	15	One Less Bell To Answer† (Marilyn McCoo, lead vocal)	Bell
3/13/71	19	8	Love's Lines, Angles & Rhymes (Marilyn McCoo, lead vocal)	Bell
10/2/71	12	9	Never My Love (Marilyn McCoo, lead vocal)	Bell
1/29/72	37	3	Together Let's Find Love	Bell
4/22/72	8	13	(Last Night) I Didn't Get To Sleep At All† (Marilyn McCoo, lead vocal)	Bell
9/30/72	10	12	If I Could Reach You (Marilyn McCoo, lead vocal)	Bell
2/10/73	32	4	Living Together, Growing Together	Bell

**** Winner of 4 GRAMMY® awards
** Winner of 2 GRAMMY® awards
* Winner of 1 GRAMMY® award
† RIAA Certified Gold Record (million-seller)

THE MARILYN MCCOO & BILLY DAVIS, JR. SINGLES

Song Title	Date	Label
I Hope We Get To Love In Time/ There's Got To Be A Happy Ending	1976	ABC
You Don't Have To Be A Star (To Be In My Show)/ We've Got To Get It On Again*†	1976	ABC
Your Love/My Love For You (Will Always Be The Same)	1977	ABC
Look What You've Done To My Heart/In My Lifetime	1977	ABC
Wonderful/Hard Road Down	1977	ABC
My Reason To Be Is You/The Two Of Us	1977	ABC
Shine On Silver Moon/I Got The Words, You Got The Music	1978	Columbia
12" Shine On Silver Moon/I Got The Words, You Got The Music	1978	Columbia

THE MARILYN MCCOO & BILLY DAVIS, JR. ALBUMS

Album Title	Date	Label
I Hope We Get To Love In Time	1976	ABC
The Two Of Us	1977	ABC
Marilyn & Billy	1978	Columbia